# Body [in] Parts

# Body [in] Parts

## Bodies and Identity in Sade and Guibert

## Clara Orban

Lehigh
University
Press

Bethlehem: Lehigh University Press

Associated University Presses
2010 Eastpark Boulevard
Cranbury, NJ 08512

The paper used in this publication meets the requirements of the American National Standard for Permanence of Paper for Printed Library Materials Z39.48-1984.

Library of Congress Cataloging-in-Publication Data

Orban, Clara Elizabeth, 1960–
    Body [in] parts : bodies and identity in Sade and Guibert / Clara Orban.
        p.   cm.
    Includes bibliographical references and index.
    ISBN 978-0-934223-97-3 (alk. paper)
    1. Sade, marquis de, 1740–1814--Criticism and interpretation.   2. Guibert, Hervé--Criticism and interpretation.   3. Body, Human, in literature.
    I. Title.   II. Title: Body parts.
    PQ2063.S3O73  2008
    843'.6--dc22                                                              2007038505

# Contents

# Acknowledgments

IN 1993, I TAUGHT A COMPARATIVE LITERATURE COURSE ON "IMAGES OF Disease in Literature." A colleague, Pascale-Anne Brault, introduced me to the work of an author on whom she was working, Hervé Guibert, who died of AIDS in 1991. She lent me a copy of his text *Cytomégalovirus: Journal d'Hospitalisation.* The journal so impressed me that I distributed my translation to the class as one of the readings for the course. I would like to thank those students especially for challenging me to explain Guibert to them. I also thank students I have taught since then who have read bits of Guibert and brought fresh ideas to test. In 1996, I had the translation published. Pascale-Anne Brault's continued support, careful reading of this project, and insightful comments on my work have provided invaluable help.

I would like to thank the DePaul University College of Liberal Arts and Sciences for a summer grant that allowed me to begin collecting information on both Guibert and Sade. A leave of absence from teaching and service responsibilities thanks to DePaul University's University Research Council allowed me to finish the manuscript.

Many colleagues and friends have contributed to this book in many ways. Without Kevin J. Harty's encouragement and comments on presentations I did on Guibert over several years and at various venues, I might not have pursued Guibert this far. Andrew Suozzo's suggestions on the text have helped clarify my readings on Guibert and Sade. His deep understanding of eighteenth century ideas and writers and his subtle reading of Sade's role as Enlightenment writer and intellectual helped clarify my perspectives throughout this text. Gary Cestaro's suggestions for theoretical readings helped bridge gaps in my understanding of frameworks pertinent to Guibert's work. His careful comments on an early draft of this text have at times been incorporated here. Adam Hilevski's contribution to honing my reading of Sade,

7

especially, greatly focused the text. Suzanne Poirier, who published an early article I wrote on Guibert, gave excellent advice to help shape my ideas on Guibert. I am fortunate to call these colleagues friends.

Many thanks to Ralph Sarkonak for his swift answer to my question about Sade and Guibert. DePaul's library staff did an excellent job of sleuthing out Sade's letters when editions seemed impossible to find. I am indebted also to the anonymous reader of the press whose comments reshaped my chapters. Judi Mayer and Scott Paul Gordon of Lehigh University Press, and Christine Retz of Associated University Presses, have offered great encouragement and timely assistance throughout the process of completing this manuscript. This study has benefited from the generosity of all these individuals.

As always: to Elliot.

*      *      *

I gratefully acknowledge the following presses for allowing me to quote passages from their works: Cornell University Press, Peter Cryle, *Geometry in the Boudoir. Configurations of French Erotic Narrative* (1994); Éditions Gallimard, Hervé Guibert, *Le protocole compassionnel* (1991); George Braziller, Inc., Hervé Guibert, *The Compassion Protocol*, Translated by James Kirkup (1994).

The following article provided much information and inspiration for the present study:

The Johns Hopkins University Press, *Literature and Medicine*, Clara Orban, "Writing, Time and AIDS in the Works of Hervé Guibert," 18 no. 1 (Spring 1999): 132–50. I am very grateful to Johns Hopkins University Press for allowing me to incorporate material from that article into this text.

# Body [in] Parts

# Introduction

—Two bodies entwined, a third
eye watching them
—The camera lens caressing a
naked man's body in the window, veiled light
—The right eye, troubled vision,
difficulty reading, hearing still
intact
—A patient covered in dried blood
on a gurney, a sublime body,
erotic emotions

—The body buckles under its own
weight in the X-ray room
—A pile of bodies coupling in an
immense room in the château
—A body pierced through with
needles, bleeding
—Extremities cut off for ultimate
sexual arousal; coupling with
the dying body

THESE QUOTES AND INTERPRETIVE SNIPPETS RECALL MOMENTS REPEATED
in various ways in the works of the Marquis de Sade and Hervé
Guibert. Guibert examines his body and that of others in moments of sexual abandon but also while in decline, at moments
of weakness. Sade knows no weakness: his body and those of his
characters either belong to the torturers or the victims. The bodies of the strong subjugate those of the weak; they take control
of their bodies even to the point of annihilation, making them
disappear.

A striking aspect of the works of the Marquis de Sade and
Hervé Guibert is their relentless pursuit to say everything about
the body, exploring it in ways either unsanctioned by good taste
or forbidden outright. They tell all about the body: how it con-
ceals identity, how it loses its identity, how time ravages it or ne-
glects it, and how it ultimately decays and disappears. Guibert's
works owe more than a passing, anecdotal debt to those of Sade,
for both explore the body to excruciating limits.

A primary impetus for this project comes from my belief that
Hervé Guibert's works have not received the attention they de-
serve. For English-speaking readers, literary scholarship on his

works is still somewhat limited. Partially, this is due to the lack of a complete translation of his literary production into English to allow readers to know his work fully. Of Guibert's works, his AIDS texts were translated first. Early on, they were wildly popular both in France and among French-speaking readers. However, translations of Guibert into English do not include works from all periods of his literary production. Less than half his works have been translated thus far. Guibert texts published after 1988 are accessible in translation, while his shorter works are not.[1] Similarly, besides several notable exceptions, such as a few book-length scholarly analyses and several important articles, critics have largely ignored Guibert.[2] This leaves a gap to fill. Guibert remains one of the most important writers of his generation, as well as a major gay writer in France.

A striking omission in analysis is the intertextual relationship between Guibert and the Marquis de Sade, an influence partially hidden in the textual shadows, partially boldly acknowledged. In many ways, Sade and Guibert explored the same mental universe: the recess of the human psyche. This connection needs to be elaborated to better understand Guibert and, I hope, to shed light on Sade as well.

Virtually every "great thinker" in France has grappled with the implications of the marquis's negation of universal good. After a century and a half of piecemeal textual *retrouvailles* in drafty attics, dusty basements, and forgotten corners of libraries, Sade's works became available in Gilbert Lely's complete edition (1962–1967).[3] Especially during the twentieth century and since then, French intellectuals have discussed the implications of Sade's reversal of Enlightenment paradigms. Guibert is one of these intellectuals. But instead of confronting Sade, approaching his works as documents to be interpreted for a scholarly audience, Guibert incorporates Sade into his own works. The *corps*—staged, brutalized, destroyed, and so cruelly laid out for us in Sade—comes into Guibert's text as the body unmasked, sexually fantasized, and diseased.

Bodies in Guibert's texts undergo a loss of identity, which leads to disintegration of the body into its phantom image.[4] Initially, identity remains hidden, masked as a means of sexual play, sexual predation, or sexual orientation. Subsequently, the young body loses its identity through disease. The strategies Guibert uses to explore identity and body construction and deconstruction owe much to Sade's influence.

This exploration of Guibert through Sade brings a body of evidence to bear on the ways bodies lose their corporality.

Another reason for the comparatively scarce critical literature on Guibert may be the discomfort many of his texts produce in the reader, with their allusions to deviant sexuality and their ambiguous narrative, the autofictional voice that narrates shocking acts.[5] Guibert's work presents a challenge to the reader and the critic, as do the works of the libertine who inspired him. This connection between Guibert and Sade may help elucidate the unflinching tone of Guibert's works.

Unlike the dearth of critical literature on Guibert, Sade has been the object of almost one hundred years of intense study in France and elsewhere. In some sense, tackling Sade seems to have been a rite of passage for every French intellectual since the Second World War. Once rescued from obscurity—many of Sade's texts vanished during the French Revolution, only to reappear either in private hands or in the bowels of the Bibliothèque Nationale during the early part of the twentieth century—literary surrealism embraced the transgressive nature of the newly found texts. Moreover, once Sade's works were assembled for the first time, scholarly interest boomed. In fact, analyzing and reinterpreting Sade became the privilege of men and women of letters during the last half century of the 1900s—Jacques Lacan, Georges Bataille, Pier Paolo Pasolini, Roland Barthes, Simone de Beauvoir, Gilles Deleuze, and Jane Gallop.[6] Sade came to represent the supreme iconoclast, the limits of critical discourse and rationality. Philosophers, artists, psychoanalysts, and critics turned to Sade and grappled with him, perhaps as a way to test their own limits.[7]

Much of the fascination with Sade comes from the contrast between his works and those of his contemporaries. Sade represents the negative image of the Age of Enlightenment. He allows us to see how reason can be pushed to its limits, distorted and manipulated. The existence of writers such as Sade, and to a lesser extent Denis Diderot or Rétif de la Bretonne, explodes the notion of a unified search for ideal rationalism among French eighteenth-century thinkers. The *philosophes* sought to examine the human condition, morality, man's place in the cosmos, and metaphysical possibilities. They did not always conclude that man was universally good. An ironic, often somewhat cynical perspective on human nature appears in a work such as Voltaire's *Candide,* perhaps the quintessential narrative of universal ratio-nalism. Candide, of course, after searching the world for his true love, Cunégonde, finds her, but she is no longer the ideal of beauty and purity to which he aspired. He concludes his search by retrenching to his own plot of land, for we must each cultivate our individual gardens. The mind's limitations cannot, in the end, understand rationally ideals of beauty and truth. We must live life on more practical grounds. But we continue to search for those ideals nonetheless, for it is the human condition.

Sade begins his search from the perspective that ideals are not noble. We seek pleasure, often at all costs. Sade brings the same empirical, rational framework to bear on the pursuit of sexual gratification as the philosophes do on higher ideals.[8]

When comparing more contemporary authors to Sade, their willingness to address Sade's thought reflects on the authors themselves. That Lacan, Bataille, and de Beauvoir, for example, all tackled Sade's works brings to the fore intricacies of the phi-losophies and theories of the twentieth-century thinkers. Sade becomes a touchstone, a rite of passage for the intellectual intent on exploring all, on saying all. Sade himself used the expression "tout dire" to characterize his literary ambitions. So, too, does writing about Sade mean trying to explore the limits of analysis.[9]

One of the most striking aspects of Guibert is his literary debt to Sade. Not only are Guibert's texts filled with transgressive sex-uality—suggestions of pedophilia, orgies, and other sexual sce-narios calculated to shock bourgeois sensibilities—but the title of one of his works from the mid-1980s, *Vous m'avez fait former des fantômes (You Have Made Me Form Phantoms),* is taken from Sade. In a letter from July 1783, Sade wrote to his wife, "For ex-ample, you fancied you were sure to work wonders, I'll wager, by reducing me to an atrocious abstinence in the article of *carnal sin.* Well, you were wrong; you have produced a ferment in my brain, owing to you phantoms have arisen in me which I shall have to render real."[10]

Guibert found another connection between his work and that of the marquis. In one of Guibert's last texts, *Le Protocole com-passionnel (The Compassion Protocol),* he alludes to Sade. In this novel, a continuation of the exposition of the ravages of AIDS on his ailing, dying body, Guibert hopes a new treatment will help him while he reflects on and continues his writing. In a centrally located chapter, he compares the voyage through time AIDS forces his body to undertake to childhood fables. He, a 35-year-old, has the body of a 95-year-old, as though the world projected forward to the year 2050. In this way, he sees himself closer to his great-aunt Suzanne, since aunt and nephew can communicate through their aging bodies. Moreover, it seems that, because of his physical decline, his parents have become his children. His body's weakness becomes visible to those he meets. But a DDI treatment procured from a dancer who died of AIDS before the treatment could take effect has revitalized him somewhat. His body's newfound, although limited, strength leads Guibert to reflect on the notion of "goodness," as interpreted in the gesture of the anonymous dancer who may be prolonging his life. Guibert seems shocked, therefore, that David, a friend of his, declares Guibert "méchant." David points out "you know your own books, don't you?,"[11] suggesting cruelty has been a theme in Guibert's writing. Before his readers, Guibert denies the charge; his texts have been crisscrossed by truth and lies, by treason, by the theme of cruelty, but not a fundamental cruelty. He concludes, "I do not think any good work of art can ever be unkind. Sade's celebrated principle of delicacy. I have the feeling I've created a work both barbarous and delicate."[12] With works at once barbarous and delicate, literature both good and evil, Guibert suggests literary acts of cruelty are only superficially so, for literature balances between two poles.

The "celebrated principle of delicacy" noted here refers to another letter Sade sent his wife only months after the letter quoted previously. Between November 23–24, 1783, Sade wrote to his wife:

> Charming creature, you want my soiled linen, my old linen? Were you aware that 'tis the epitome of refinement? You see how I can separate the wheat from the chaff. Listen, my angel, I would like nothing better than to satisfy you on this score, for you know full well that I respect peoples' tastes and their fantasies; no matter how seemingly strange or odd they might be, I find them all respectable, both because we are not their masters and because when you take a really close look

at even the most peculiar and the most bizarre of them, they always emanate from some principle of sensitivity.[13]

In the July letter, he rails to his wife against his captivity and its limitations. In particular, he lashes out at "the gentlemen," his captors, who have denied his request to receive a copy of Jean-Jacques Rousseau's *Confessions* despite having allowed him to read Lucretius and Voltaire. Sade says that Rousseau would provide him impetus to improve himself. Denying him reading material proves counterproductive, because one must often tolerate evil to destroy vice. Therefore, carnal abstinence has not healed his debauchery; on the contrary, it has produced phantoms, stoked his imagination, a great Sadean paradox.

The second letter begins with a sarcastic query about the marquise's interest in bed linens. It reads as a sort of manifesto of liberation of fantasies, for there, the bizarre and the sensitive meet. With its almost poetic use of nicknames for his wife and its anecdotes, the November letter seems almost a literary endeavor. Both letters set up paradoxes by opposing terms in oxymoronic fashion: on the one hand two nouns, *abstinence* and *fantasies*, on the other two adjectives, *bizarre* and *sensitive*. Paradox will be at the heart of the seduction the libertine's work exerts on the young author.

We must consider Guibert's adoption of these two passages from Sade because they shed light on Sade's influence on his work in a larger sense. We know Guibert had read Gilbert Lely's biography of Sade because he mentions it in *Le Mausolée des amants*, his journal from 1976 to 1991 published in 2001. One morning, as Guibert finished Lely's text, he feels rested. "I have the impression of physiologic well being, calm, I feel my body full of shit and I know that I'll be able to get rid of it."[14] He continues, "Sade draws the dream topography of an establishment of desire: the rooms of shame and of torture open simply into a cemetery."[15] His journal mentions his text *Vous m'avez fait former des fantômes* shortly after these reflections on Sade, so presumably Lely's biography spurred Guibert's interest in writing a novel inspired by one of the marquis's maxims. However, since references to Sade in Guibert's journal are sparse, he probably had his interest in the libertine's work reinforced by Barthes.

As Guibert's biographer François Buot reminds us, Guibert and

Barthes had a complex relationship. Guibert admired Barthes's work and sent him a copy of *La Mort propagande* (*Propaganda Death*).[16] In an interview with Didier Eribon, Guibert mentions that Barthes approached him to begin a conversation conducted via letters on the relationship between writing and "le fantasme."[17] In fact, Barthes's final reflection on Sade in his study *Sade, Fourier, Loyola* comes back to the idea of *délicatesse,* (sensitivity). Barthes understands Sade's ideas in this letter from November 1783 as emblematic of a particular way all of Sade's work can be read: as a plan of violence, but also according to a "principle of tact."[18] Tact, délicatesse, becomes less a product of style and civility than the power of analysis and a means of ejaculation together, an exaltation that constitutes utopia. While the language of violence follows an age-old path, Sade's délicatesse constitutes a new language destined to subvert. We can see that this reading of Sade's letter may very well have had a profound impact on Guibert's understanding of the marquis. Language becomes subversive pleasure.

Sade becomes an inspiration for Guibert also through association with Barthes. We can see here several interrelated strands come together: desire, phantoms, traces of discourse, pleasure, delicacy, violence, and writing. Sade's work alludes to connections between these elements, Barthes recognizes these links, and Guibert used Sade's reflections as a model for many of his own literary visions.

For Guibert, Sade's works could serve as models for his own because they propose a world not of black and white, but nuanced and morally ambiguous. When Guibert acknowledges a literary debt to Sade through the stylistic concern for barbarous subjects presented in morally neutral, even delicate ways, he implicitly embraces the marquis's vision of the body. It is bodies that undergo barbarous and unspeakable treatment in Sade's works. And yet Sade speaks of tortured bodies in a way that, by its very balanced and calculated form, seems to conform to social convention. Sade describes horrors without seeming horrified. In his reference to Sade, Guibert suggests that acts of cruelty, when related without hysteria, may seem rational. From here, perhaps, comes the understanding that Guibert has of his own works' delicacy and barbarous nature.

The inclusion of a reference to Sade here is central to understanding Guibert's sense of the epistemological weight of his ideas. Guibert's understanding of Sade recalls Nietzschean ideals of boundaries not only blurred but also overcome in a literary terrain beyond morality. Sade and Guibert meet in the works of the philosopher who lived in a time between them both. Although Sade may be anticipating Nietzsche in his creation of a literature enacting a reversal of Enlightenment philosophical ideas, Guibert's texts do not strive either to support or combat philosophical principles.

More so than a moral or amoral approach to the human condition, Sade and Guibert share an idea of the body's use and usefulness, of identity, and the disintegration of both. In these authors, identity does not identify. At various moments of his life, Sade modified his name, often to better adapt to new political realities when a recognizable aristocratic moniker became uncomfortable. He often denied his scandalous adventures, trying to remain anonymous, hidden from public scrutiny. In his texts as well, characters routinely lose identities, hide identities, adopt new ones, and wear or discard masks, often as ways to enhance or accelerate situations of potential sexual satisfaction. Guibert, too, denied or denigrated his biography, often ridiculing his bourgeois upbringing through stinging criticism of his parents and betrayal of friends.[19] He was widely criticized for "unmasking" friends and lovers, many of whom, it was presumed, wished not to have their sexual orientation revealed. In his texts as well, characters mask and unmask, conceal identity, go unnamed, and provide biographical information that at times is contradicted later in the text. In both authors, identities are shifting markers, mere constructions of the self.

What's more, shifting identity implies more than creation of new selves. It implicates the author's narrative stance. Authorial narrative voices lose their configuration as Guibert denies and accepts responsibility for his texts. He assumes a mask, but lets it drop enough for the reader to view the author in the background. And as Guibert's texts shift focus toward the dying body, a new identity of an old man, of a disappearing self takes over. As Isabelle Décarie states, the gesture of masking "is inherent to all discourse concerning death."[20] The masks that hide identity as a way of creating new selves become indispensable as one speaks of death. Even assuming responsibility for words becomes a strategy for control. In an analysis of dialogue and power, David Caron explains Guibert's use of speech modes and how it relates not only to power but also inevitably to his sexual orientation. "In Guibert's text, gossip provides queer readers with a familiar mode of communication: gossip has been for many of us an inevitable and even vital activity."[21] Through language, identity and identification shift, and discursive strategies realign affiliation.[22]

Sade and Guibert meet where the body becomes all-powerful. They also construct literary landscapes where bodies fall apart. For Raymond Bellour, Guibert creates "a sort of mythology, an epic vision of the body and its impulses."[23] The dark side of this mythical vision exists in Sade as well. In both authors, bodies inevitably succumb to a process that destroys them, to a disarticulation through violence for Sade or through disease for Guibert. In both authors, this disarticulation is also absence of speech or fear of losing the ability to construct dialogue. In Sade, characters are spared so they can tell their tales. If one does not articulate, one is disarticulated in his texts. In Guibert, disease risks leaving him unable to write or to speak, which becomes the primary concern as his body betrays him. Not being able to speak, not being able to write, and being cut up form a nexus of intersecting imageries in these two authors.

Once identities shift and multiply and hide from the bodies to which they were linked, what becomes of the body itself? In an examination of the body's materiality, Judith Butler notes, "What constitutes the fixity of the body, its contours, its movements, will be fully material, but materiality will be rethought as the effect of power, as power's most productive effect."[24] She further understands performativity, the linguistic act that, according to Austin, creates and gives materiality to language, not as "the act by which a subject brings into being what she/he names, but, rather, as that reiterative power of discourse to produce the phenomena that it regulates and constrains."[25] Butler redefines *sex;* it is not determined a priori in the material body, but, just as gender in Butler's terms, it is somewhat constructed. The construction of the body, its materiality, and its existence as matter come partially through language. Bodies, in both Sade and Guibert, are not fixed constructions. Bodies do not remain linked to their identities, and, once adrift, the body becomes vulnerable to manipulation by others. Sade's torturers exploit the anonymity of

some of their victims; Guibert's disease becomes his identity as
he navigates the hospital. So bodies undergo modifications,
largely, as Butler suggests, because of shifting power relationships. Torturers, doctors, sexual contraptions, and medical ma-
chinery all manipulate the bodies in their control because they
have the hierarchical or physical power to do so. Each modifica-
tion of bodies in Sade and Guibert entails a concomitant shift in
the language to describe the body. The ultimate result of this dynamic process of identification and materiality in both authors is
the disappearance of bodies. For both Sade and Guibert, bodies
ultimately become immaterial—not just disarticulated but disin-
tegrated.

For implicit in the discussion of the body's materiality is the
possibility of the body's physical disarticulation. A sense of identity may be dependent on a physical body to possess it, but what
if the body itself, through powerlessness as Butler might suggest,
is disarticulated? In Sade, time never passes, in endless bliss or
endless pain. The mutilations are staged in theatrical settings
and scenarios. Bodies are imprisoned, and victims are raped,
mutilated, and ultimately bled to death for the sexual gratification of all-powerful torturers.

Guibert's bodies relinquish power or are overpowered by lovers, by friends, and, in fictional scenarios, by gangsters, thieves,
and strangers. His own body loses its battle against time, succumbing to AIDS. The body takes center stage, too, as Guibert
records sexual exploits and limitations and reveals the secrets of
others. Bodies are imprisoned and dying of AIDS, Guibert's body
itself becomes a prison. Before the body disintegrates, to become
phantom, the writer breathes one last bit of life into it through
writing. In Guibert, as in Sade, only telling a story saves: writing,
narrating until the end.

Guibert and Sade used their own worlds and their own lives as
backdrop for their texts. What is lived, or what the public believes
is lived, becomes interwoven with the fabric of the text. Biography and autobiography, with presumptions of truth-telling and
narrative linearity, are disrupted in Guibert especially as his biography becomes his fiction. In the first chapter of this study, "Irresistible Biographies," I explore the ways in which both writers
bring the realities of their experience to the text, weaving them

so tightly into the cloth of their fantasies and their nightmares that it is often difficult to distinguish the beginnings and the ends of the reality.

One of the main points of convergence between the works of the two authors is their desire to unmask sexuality. Sade gave his name to sexual deviance, and Guibert's textual sexuality often also alludes to the transgressive sexuality inspired by Sade. Intercourse becomes a form of defiance. It also by necessity must become part of an exteriorization of the self for the consumption of others. In this way it resembles the theater, where masks, disguises, and interchangeable personae consume the "reality" of the presentation and substitute for it. This follows from the type of masking/unmasking that was at work in the reworking of biographies to become fiction. In the second chapter, "Sexual Performance: Staging and Watching Bodies in the Act," I explore how Sade's transgressive sexuality becomes a model for Guibert's, and how both in truth stem from the same impulse to shock.

Time regulates the body's ability to inhabit space in Einsteinian, paradoxical fashion. The continuum on which the body projects itself leads to accelerated decay. Bodies inevitably are destroyed because of time. Masking the body, or at least attempting mastery of it through literature, necessitates taking control of time. The linear text can be twisted to deny, at least temporarily, the flow of time inherent in narrative structure. Sade's texts control time and use the calendar to shape bodily appropriations. Tortures seem more acute to the victims because time never passes, it is only infinitely measured in slow ticks. Guibert manipulates explicit temporal constructs to deny time its inexorable control of the body's decay. Through simulated journals and diaries, Guibert demarcates everything that happens to his body, which keeps it alive in the text. Chapter 3, "Counting the Days: Hiding and Seeking to Pass the Time," explores how time becomes a weapon both against and for the body, enemy and ally.

Imprisonment also primes bodies for torture. The prelude to the body's disappearance is the enclosure that does not allow it to move. Being imprisoned and then going free only to be enclosed again constitute the primary movement of Sade's texts, with escape often a futile attempt at freedom. Yet the storytellers—those who survive because they can tell stories or those who

have survived years of torture to tell their tales—gain a measure
of freedom by the very act of telling. In Guibert's texts, too, bodies of victims are imprisoned, blindness limits the body's freedom, and the decaying body succumbing to disease remains
imprisoned within itself. Often, only the act of writing can allow
the mind to be free. In the fourth chapter, "Imprisoned Bodies/
Liberating Narratives," I discuss images of prisons in both writers
and how telling stories brings freedom. Ultimately, the healthy
body disappears in Guibert's works over time, just as Sade's anti-
heroes' victims' bodies disappear under the whip or the knife. I
will look at the dynamic of the imprisoned body in the works of
both authors and the ways in which telling stories, writing, becomes the only way to be free.

The body—the locus of the tale, of the writer's view of the
world, and of the biography behind the tale—appears fragmented in the works of these two authors. In several of Sade's
texts, the bodies of the victims undergo progressive laceration
and then dismemberment as the tortures perpetrated on their
bodies increase in intensity to satisfy the increasing lust of the
torturers. The body cannot appear before the reader but must be
pieced together, just as the reality of the text must sometimes be
surmised. Also in the works of these authors where disease, torture, and death abound, a ghostly presence hovers over the texts.
At the end of Sade's *Cent Vingt Journées de Sodome, ou l'école du
libertinage* (*The 120 Days of Sodom*), the impending dismantling
of the castle, which represents the doomed Ancien Régime, a political system that created and nurtured the torturers, accelerates
the progressive disappearance of victims.[26] In Guibert, the photograph—the visual image on camera, the ghostly reflection of the
image on film—mirrors the body as it vanishes due to disease. In
the fifth chapter, "Disappearing Act: Bodies Dissected, Ghostly
Remains," I examine the nature of dismemberment as a trope in
the works of Sade and then compare it to the disembodied bodies
and the dying body of the AIDS victim akin to the old body of his
relatives or of other characters in Guibert's work. I then look at
the image of the ghost, at photographs and film, to see how
seeing and not seeing converge.

The concept *pudeur*—modesty, decency, even shame—moves
to the center of Guibert's discourse on the body. In his texts filled
with audacious gestures by children or adults, *impudeur*—

indecency, shamelessness, immodesty—toward bodies is veiled in an aura of upright social behavior and sober language. As is the case for Sade, whose prose is both covert and discreet, all the while describing obscenities, in Guibert, extreme gestures are described in language calculated to seem modest, even sober.

Transgression becomes a game for Guibert, a way to push respectability to its limits. More than merely the desire to "épater les bourgeois" so dear to surrealists, among others, transgression becomes a way of marking difference, of creating a new identity as Other. As was the case for Sade, transgression can and does take place through language. Satisfying the urge to "say everything" constitutes transgression through language. In Sade's case, the text is also infused with the light irony, the literary mockery dear to the eighteenth century. Guibert's linguistic impudeur reveals itself through frank discussion of the body, language not sustained by metaphor or euphemism. Language becomes clinical and anatomical, dissecting the reality of the body in a methodical way reminiscent, perhaps, of medical discourse. Guibert shows us what is possible, just as Sade's unbridled sexual perversions were described within a rational framework. For Buot, "in Guibert, there is a jubilation linked to physical pleasure of which he speaks with ease and that he associates with suffering. Hervé knows well the Sadean vision of the world."[27] The issue in both authors is that bodies lose their corporeality. They are denied a history through shifting biographies and autobiographies; they lose their physical reality in time; they are objectified and mechanized as a way of dehumanizing them; they are cut up, imprisoned; and they become ghosts who haunt the texts. Bodies take center stage in these two authors. Guibert does indeed know Sade's world well, its pleasure linked to suffering, grounded in bodies that lose their identities and ultimately disappear.

# 1

## Irresistible Biographies

CREATING IDENTITY MEANS COMING TO AN UNDERSTANDING OF, COMING to terms with, the body, its materiality, spatial dimensions, sexuality, and physical limitations. It also means, for Charles Taylor and others, finding sources of the self in a moral dimension. But first, identity resides in a sense of corporeality. As Butler suggests, the body first establishes itself as a material entity with a presence. With that materiality comes an understanding of the psychic, social, cultural, and other factors that allow the body to inhabit the physical space it occupies. In many ways, identity forms when materiality comes to terms with its surroundings. The body becomes more than a *corps;* it creates a corpus of understanding when it becomes contextualized. Having an identity means also acknowledging a biography, establishing a historical narrative of where the body has been. That is not to suggest that biography and identity are one and the same. As a genre, biography is of course fraught with elements that limit its truth value: authorial presence, theoretical frameworks, selection of narrative sequences and so forth. What I mean here is that a material body has a lived history that becomes its biography, the narrative of its materiality. At times, just as is the case with the literary biographical genre, the narrative is shaped less by actual occurrences than by narrative strategy. In this chapter, I retrace both Sade and Guibert's biographies to uncover how they developed as writers. I then look at some ways in which their writings, often about themselves, both revealed and concealed their identities.

In his biography of Sade, Lawrence Bongie established that biography and writing feed off each other; the scandal created by one is amplified by the other. That is why he speaks of biography as an irresistible force, a term alluded to in the chapter title here. Biography in some ways cannot be concealed—it can get away from you. Michel Delon notes that Sade was credited with several crimes he never committed, such as murder, because the reading public began to assume that his works contained autobiographical details. His writings became, in some ways, his biography. Furthermore, Sade's work reveals a certain amount of autobiographical intertextuality; Sade can claim to be the philosopher in the boudoir, expounding rationally on pleasure and pain. At times text and life become one, and the two together become something beyond both.

Guibert's texts, too, are at once autobiographies and fiction, autofictions, a term introduced in the preceding chapter. For Jean-Pierre Boulé, "like Montaigne, [Guibert] is always the subject of his works"[1] His texts are filled with veiled and not-so-veiled references to acquaintances, friends, and family members whom, as Worton noted, Guibert betrayed. Sexuality, death, and the desire to write continue to weave together. For Guibert, the photographic camera and the video camera also provide opportunities for relentless self-portraits. For both authors, their styles of writing about perversions are calculated on the *moi,* the "I," a mythic doubling of the self. Autobiography and fiction intertwine to create a persona both apparent and hidden from view.

In many ways, both Guibert and Sade provide clues in their biographies of the writers they would become. "Biographies" themselves are transgressive in the works of both authors. They use life facts when it suits their literary, philosophical, or exclamatory purposes while concealing details when convenient. Both Guibert and Sade allow their biographies to infiltrate their texts without overtly calling the genre in which they work an autobiography. The blurring of the real and the fictional becomes one of the key strategies used by both authors to hide and to highlight the nature of the illusive—and illusionary—nature of the text. Their biographies follow as a way to understand the reality on which their fiction is based. The self and the body shift parameters as identity takes its shape.

## IDENTITY AND SEXUALITY

It is not possible to fully explore Guibert or, to a certain extent, Sade without a discussion of sexual identity. A fully formed self

depends on a thoroughly grounded sense of sexual identity and
orientation. Through the ages, the terminology used to describe
same-sex desire has shifted. Sanctions against homosexual practice have also fluctuated depending on political and ecclesiastical
climates and mandates. Many studies of homosexuality in Europe, for example, propose historical chronologies for shifts in
terminology and penalties and for rejection or acceptance of homosexuality. As one of the key components of identity, a sense of
sexual identity contributes greatly to an individual's conceptions
of his or her own body.

For Guibert, certainly, his homosexuality defined his life and
his works. As an adolescent in the late 1960s, Guibert benefited
fully from the general loosening of societal mores with regard to
homosexuality. He was also caught in the ignorance and scientific obfuscation surrounding transmission of HIV and AIDS in
the early years of the pandemic. As he confronts AIDS in his later
texts, he recalls lovers who may also have infected him. Sexual
orientation becomes a primary marker of body identification for
Guibert.

For Sade, the issue is more problematic. To be identified as homosexual in Sade's society, of course, carried with it many reper-
cussions, beginning with alienation and a personal sense of
Otherness with respect to heterosexuality. Sade's texts are replete
with descriptions of anal intercourse and homoerotic encounters, especially in orgiastic scenes. In today's terminology, we
would say Sade's biography indicates he was bisexual. At the
time, legal and societal discourse on same-sex desire, especially
male-to-male desire, used the term *sodomy*. The focus of this
term is on the act itself, not the agent. Practicing anal intercourse
rather than vaginal was the key factor in defining sexual identity.
Today, by using words such as homosexual or bisexual, the desires of the agent are privileged, whether the agent is male or female. In terms of a politics of the body, rather than evoke the
ways in which bodies are used during intercourse, implicit in the
term sodomy, the terms *homosexual* and *bisexual* denote the objects of desire that define sexual orientation. A brief understanding of same-sex desire will allow us to better capture both Sade
and Guibert's understanding of how their own sexualities shaped
and contributed to their identities.

Sodomy was considered a capital crime in many parts of Europe. Although punishment was unequally meted out at different times and in different places, the practice was condemned by the Church. Yet, something begins to change in European under-standing of sodomy several decades before Sade's birth. Of the Renaissance, Lever states, "The liberation of homosexuality—or more exactly of bisexuality—constitutes one of the most spectac-ular victories. But it only profited the elite: the king and his court, artists of renown, and a few intellectuals."[2]

Equally provocative is Randolph Trumbach's analysis of the shifting nature of societal understanding of same-sex desire in the years beginning in 1700. First of all, he writes, "The behavior and status of women were being modified by new ideals of ro-mantic marriage, conjugal companionship, and the tender care of children. But the behavior and status of men were more mark-edly transformed by the new meaning attached to sexual rela-tions between males." In northwestern Europe before 1700, he notes, sexual relations between adult men and adolescent boys were common, although frowned on by the Church.[3] Sex be-tween adult males and boys, and by extension other men, only became stigmatized when relations between the sexes and re-definitions of gender roles came into play in this period. This new idea of marriage probably changed the role of men. Trumbach tells us that European society had begun to move from one to the other of the two worldwide systems for organizing homosexual behavior: from a system in which "subordination was achieved by difference in age to one whose focus was a third-gender role for a minority of men."[4]

David Caron notes that the term homosexual appeared for the first time in Germany in 1869 as a more tolerant alternative to the morally tainted *sodomite*.[5] This is not to suggest that sodomy was an accepted practice immune to criminal sanction during Sade's day.[6] Police hired boys called *mouches* (stool pigeons) to assist in arrests for sodomy. The *mouche* was usually a former prostitute hired to catch pederasts and to arrest them in flagrante delicto. Michel Rey reminds us that, in his memoirs, the police lieutenant general Lenoir estimated at 20,000 the number of Parisian sod-omites,[7] so that "by 1715, two officers were working full-time tracking Parisian sodomites."[8] In terms of punishment for sod-omy, just before the Revolution, "all those who seemed suscepti-ble to disseminating the vice (by debauching young men or by

organizing prostitution) were sent to the Hospital General of Bicêtre, south of Paris. Those who were wealthier paid for their own
stay there. One could be released by displaying consistent signs
of repentance. The police returned foreigners to their own coun-
tries, and sent provincials back to their regions of origin."[9]

To some extent, the legal system responded to this shift in understanding of gender roles and the body. First of all, it was more
difficult to prove sodomy had been perpetrated than to prove
many other crimes. Theo van der Meer says, "One of the main
legal problems the court confronted in these cases was the fact
that sodomy left no traces. There was no corpus delicti. To condemn a suspect, his confession was vital."[10] For that reason,
through time, prosecution for sodomy also became less frequent.
In Enlightenment France, Lever concludes that in the wake of the
powerful movement of ideas that marks the end of the eighteenth
century, the repression of homosexuality seemed like an anach-
ronism inherited from the absolute monarchy. Although during
this period several individuals were burned at the stake for com-
mitting sodomy, with the Revolution, sodomy laws fell progressively into disuse. The penal code of 1791 does not even mention
crimes against nature.[11] Gert Hekma adds that the eighteenth
century was a key age for the revision of ideas on sodomy and
for the self-awareness of sodomites, especially in northwestern
Europe.[12] He also notes the importance of Sade within the context of the Enlightenment in redefining, or perhaps rethinking,
sexual identity. Sade was an exception to the philosophes' politics of the body:

> He based his political philosophy precisely on sodomy. In the En-
> lightenment "the great chain of being," divine law, was being sun-
> dered, and reason and nature were becoming the cornerstones of
> social philosophy and social life. Sade radicalized this philosophy of
> rational and natural law by questioning whether prostitution, mur-
> der, theft, or sodomy were truly contrary to nature or reason. He ar-
> gued that waste was within the normal course of things, so that
> wastage of semen was in accordance with nature. There was no pur-
> pose inherent in nature or social life, he argued, so there was no need
> to link sexuality to propagation. Sade used sodomy as a particularly
> good example of that which seemed to be unnatural, unreasonable,
> and purposeless, but which could in no way be proven to be against
> nature or reason.[13]

For Hekma, Sade's *La Philosophie dans le boudoir* (*Philosophy in the Boudoir*) (1795) was an apology for the decriminalization of pederasty and sodomy. Sade emphasized that there were no rational arguments against any form of sexual behavior—prostitution, murder motivated by passion, or sodomy—and he strongly opposed the suggestion that theft, prostitution, sodomy, or "lust" murder were against nature. Sade's revision of sexual identity worked against "natural law" as put forward by the Church as well as by the *philosophes.* In his literary works, he wrote extensively about sodomy as a supreme act of pleasure, for example, in *The 120 Days of Sodom.* In this respect, he was even more radical than any apologist either of platonic Eros or of homosexual love.[14]

For both Guibert and Sade, sexuality largely creates identity. For both, transgression and freedom define how they approach desire. Sade stands out from other thinkers and writers of his age in France. His philosophy, although reasoned in a manner shaped by the seventeenth and eighteenth centuries' balanced style, creates liberty where others viewed only outlawed behavior. Sade's texts emphasize anal intercourse, both same-sex and heterosexual, as a privileged form of sexual behavior. Taking the sexual "norm" and championing its opposite puts Sade at countercurrents with his contemporaries. Sade's biography was itself a revolutionary trajectory, and the radical aspects of the life he lived become part of his work. On the terrain of the body, for Sade both biography and text come together.

## ENLIGHTENMENT AND SHADOW

In Sade's life, even his name was disguised and distorted at his birth, in a sense providing a lifelong mask for him. Donatien-Alphonse-François was to be christened Donatien-Alfonse-Louis, but only servants were present at the ceremony since neither godparents nor parents attended. The servants erroneously declared the names for the official registrar, so these "pseudonyms" became part of Sade's identity. Another incident indicative of Sade's future behavior involves the events leading to his marriage. The official registry of the presentation at court prior to his marriage (at which he was not present) lists the future

groom as Donatien Aldof François. Much later, during the Revolution, to hide the aristocratic particle in his name, Sade signed
himself "Louis Sade," a curious return to his intended given
name and certainly a cynical gesture toward the revolutionaries
in that it recalled the king's name. From the beginning, Sade's
names, his official identity, shifted as political situations and circumstances warranted.

Donatien Alphonse François Marquis Sade was born in Paris
on June 2, 1740. His father, a Provençal aristocrat whose family
tree included—at least by legendary reputation—Laura, the poet
Petrarca's muse, had been the first of his family to leave the es-
tate at La Coste near Avignon for the court in Paris. The Age of
Enlightenment provided the backdrop for the early years of the
marquis. His family connections allowed him access to the court,
and his father in particular also was in contact with Voltaire,
among others. Sade's later works, in many ways the negative
photographic image of the positivism of Enlightenment thinkers,
could only have been nurtured by a deep knowledge and subsequent aversion based on the perceived shallowness of the philosophes' optimism.[15]

Sade's licentious reputation began during his stint in the military, when word of his cruelty to prostitutes spread. His father
bailed him out of trouble several times. However, Sade's monstrous persona was largely created by four incidents that spurred
a public outcry against the abuses of the nobility.[16] The first was
Sade's mistreatment of a prostitute, Jeanne Testarde, in his
garçonnière just off the Rue Mouffetard in Paris. He brought
Testarde to his secret apartment, and there brutalized her and
profaned the crucifix in front of her. After a night of terror, he let
her go, and she promptly went to the police. The second affair,
known most often as the Arcueil Affair, involved Rose Keller. He
brought her to one of his châteaux in Arcueil and beat her.
She escaped and ran to the town, where the townspeople called
the police. Once again, public opinion magnified the affair.[17] The
third scandal, in Marseilles, involved Sade force-feeding candies
coated with Spanish fly to a group of prostitutes in his room. One
of the most damaging claims of the Marseilles incident involves
the accusation that Sade had anal intercourse with his major-
domo in the room with prostitutes drugged with Spanish fly.
Given Spanish fly's side effects,[18] though, one of the girls fell ill

and complained to the police that Sade had poisoned her. The fourth incident occurred in his château in La Coste to which he had retired. With the complicity of his wife, he established a month-long orgy with domestics hired from the village. When one of the victims escaped and reported the crimes to the police, the villagers rioted and stormed the castle. Sade escaped and returned to Paris because he had heard of his mother's impending death, but a warrant for his arrest had been outstanding in the capital. He was captured and, in 1778, began the second phase of his career: prisoner and novelist.

One of the important historical details that affected Sade's reputation was the relatively recent arrival of mass newspapers into French life. Sensational news such as Sade's case could provide fodder for the press for some time and thus spread his reputation immensely. "Nouvelles à la main," written news sheets detailing the private lives of citizens, circulated rapidly and widely, thus allowing incidents such as those in which Sade indulged to reach a wide audience. In fact, the same behavior that previously had gone relatively unpunished among aristocratic criminals was punished in Sade. Some critics argue that Sade became a scapegoat for the scandalous behavior of the nobility, and that the interest and outcry generated by his case helped further the revolutionary cause: The general public understood how much license the nobility was allowed.

Sade spent the next twelve years in several prisons and asylums in Paris. Within the walls, he produced virtually all the novels that established his reputation as a man of letters. He had always been a man of the theater who saw himself as both playwright and actor. His use of the theater's masquerade possibilities is the subject of the next chapter. In his castle, he set up a theater and produced his own plays. But the lengthy novels,— *The 120 Days of Sodom, Aline et Valcour, Justine, La Nouvelle Justine (The New Justine), Philosophy in the Boudoir,* and so forth—that stand as his contributions to anti–Enlightenment thought were all produced in prison. He often had to beg for paper and writing implements, and once wrote on a bedsheet to have his works smuggled out of prison.[19]

Sade started a new career, in some sense, as a revolutionary. He was in the Bastille during that fateful July 1789. On July 2, however, he was transferred to the former convent at Charenton

because he was considered too dangerous for the prison's vola-
tile atmosphere. He had created a disturbance among the grow-
ing crowd outside when he put his chamber pot up to an opening
in the wall to amplify his voice as he screamed to the onlookers
that prisoners' throats were being cut by guards in the Bastille,
and the people should rise up against this tyranny. So he was not
present within the prison when it was stormed. Hidden in a hole
in the wall, Sade left behind the text of *The 120 Days of Sodom*,
written on a 13-yard-long roll of paper specially ordered by his
wife. After the prison was stormed, the manuscript was recovered
and vanished for almost a century.

Sade was released from captivity in 1790 when royal arrest war-
rants were made null and void by the Revolutionary government.[20] Unlike most other aristocrats, Sade chose to stay in Paris
during the Revolution and its aftermath. He became a local rep-
resentative for the Vendôme district and wrote revolutionary
tracts for the government. This marked a tranquil period of his
life. He was, however, again imprisoned when his reputation as a
libertine, established through his texts, caught up with him during the conservative reign of Napoleon. He was incarcerated in
1801 and transferred to Charenton asylum shortly afterwards,
where he died in 1814.

In a sense, Sade rewrote his biography several times, creating
identities—libertine, victimized prisoner, harassed son-in-law—
that were read by a scandalized, but eager, public. Sade's character presents itself to the reader and the researcher as polyvalent.
He was both a literary man and a libertine, a licentious writer and
a revolutionary writer. Michel Delon describes several characteristics of the libertine. Sade:

> Plays incessantly on his double stature as aristocrat and as thinker,
> as gentleman imbued with hereditary rights and as philosopher de-
> manding new liberties . . . Sade thus became a legend, a fictitious
> being whose destiny, from generation to generation, attracts new
> narratives . . . Sade includes in his writing all the accounts of which
> he is the subject. He added voluntary imprisonment to involuntary
> imprisonment by scrutinizing social phantoms, mixed with his own.
> In his novels, he mirrors the image that public opinion threw back at
> him.[21]

Sade may not have committed all the crimes of which he was accused, but that, for Delon, is beside the point. The writings of the

libertine were so powerful that they were assumed to be based on real events. Sade became the perfect counterpoint to the Enlightenment primarily because of the content of his writings. Sade became an argument against Enlightenment philosophy because he exposed its logic. He represented a cynical perspective on the optimistic liberty exclaimed by the Encyclopedists.[22]

Sade's sexual identity, although defined by the age in which he lived, complicates the assumed definitions of sexual practices. Same-sex desire, as we have seen, was more ambiguously integrated into the sexual identities of French noblemen in the eighteenth century as a possible corollary to heterosexuality. The elite were allowed some freedom from the scandal a public account of their imprisonment on charges of sodomy would bring. Noble identities were shaped largely through affiliation with a social class, but as we have seen, their power allowed them considerable freedom in behavior, sexual and otherwise. Sade, instead, a nobleman openly prosecuted, had his sexuality publicized. In many ways, this fact consolidated his bisexuality as a component of his identity. Sade became known as a sodomite, and by championing anal intercourse in his texts, he rationalized deviance from an expected norm. Sexual identity or, for Sade, identities become a primary component of his identity. His subsequent reputation as a writer who questions the certitude of Enlightenment thought is enhanced by his reputation as licentious writer par excellence.

For this reason, then, Sade becomes a trope in his own person. He embodies the way of seeing and being about which he writes. Author and work become one. "Sade's writing alternates between articulated reason and the exacerbation of phantoms, between blasphemy and euphemism, crudeness and allusion . . . The work is thus suspended in a dynamic progression between writing and reading, and a desire that cannot be concretely satisfied."[23]

But what are the characteristics of this new language of "sadism," not just as sexual practice but also as language?

If sadism, according to its formula, is nothing more than the "vulgar content of Sade's text," the essential, from both a refined and elitist point of view, is in the grammar which organizes the poses, the episodes, the scenes, and in the invention of language capable of describing them . . . Like contemporary epistolary novels, Sade's composition implies a complicity with the reader become voyeur . . . The Encyclopedia pretended to offer the world for all to see and learn from in the form of a schematic table. Encyclopedist of evil, Sade suggests the limits of such visibility. In order to perpetuate desire, one must reinvent secret cabinets and unimaginable manias.[24]

Secrecy, hiding, and desire are part of the erotic game where ever more elaborate procedures are necessary for fulfillment.

The gesture of hiding names and erasing identity—of assuming pseudonyms to hide and to disguise—is ever prevalent in Sade's texts and is a commonplace throughout the seventeenth and eighteenth centuries. In Sade, many of the assumed names are of symbolic importance. A primary example is Sade's *120 Days of Sodom*. In brief, the story concerns four fabulously wealthy friends—three middle-aged noblemen and one clergyman—explicitly associated with the highest classes of Ancien Régime France. Their extraordinary wealth allows them to live their days in complete unbounded debauchery. They have each married daughters of one of the other friends; they have each also committed incest with these daughters. They decide to create a closed universe for their debauchery, leading them to the Castle of Silling in the "Black Forest," more a mythical secret landscape than the German territory of the same name. With them, they bring an array of victims of various degrees: male and female virgins for sacrifice, prostitutes, men specialized in sexual practices (the Four Fuckers), storytellers, cooks, and so on. They organize their four-month stay, November to March, around a highly calculated and ritualized daily existence of gargantuan eating, sexual gratification, and storytelling. As the months continue, the tortures perpetuated on victims increase, leading to their death. As the four friends prepare to leave the castle, very few of the company survive (only sixteen individuals). One of the four friends, a high-ranking man of the church, the Bishop of ***, brother of the Duc de Blangis, could not have his name associated with the intrigue of the castle of Silling. The asterisks represented a common ellipsis technique in seventeenth- and eighteenth-century novels as an ironic gesture of modesty or authorial restraint (pudeur, in Guibert's terms).

Besides this rather common literary masking, Sade also uses

pseudonyms for the other characters, but this time with a different impetus. Most of those brought to the castle against their will have their identity hidden by names referring to their duties in the castle. The "four fuckers," for example, are chosen for their extreme anatomical endowments. They were given names such as "Hercules, truly created like the god after whom he was named,"[25] "Antinoüs, thus named because, as was the case for Hadrian's bardache, he joined the most beautiful prick in the world to the most voluptuous asshole,"[26] "Ass-breaker had a prick so pleasantly contoured that it was almost impossible for him to fuck without breaking the ass,"[27] and "Jack in the Sky, thus named because his erection, no matter what he did, was perpetual."[28] These names indicate the status of the individuals in the hierarchy of violence, for not all victims have the same importance. Although all the characters have been brought to the forest hideout for the sole pleasure of the four depraved friends, some are brought because of their sexual prowess. They will in turn become victimizers of many of the weaker inhabitants. Thus, names relating to sexual power have the currency of power behind them. As Butler noted, sex, identification, and the—shifting—materiality of the body stem from a shifting relationship with power. To be named constitutes creating identity, and as Sade shows, confers hierarchical status in a nexus of power.

Other groups of victims appear only as their profession. The castle contains storytellers and cooks, two indispensable groups of people who, through their talents, allow the others to live. These groups of women satiate the physical and intellectual appetites of the four and of their victims. The storytellers are also enlisted for their sexual prowess. Only the cooks are freed of sex and servitude in the castle. So, in a sense, while the Four Fuckers satiate the sexual impulses, the other groups of "professionals" nourish other appetites in the castle.

The weakest group of victims only exists as an age and sex: young virgin boys, young virgin girls, etc. Here, the recipients of the most deviant behavior are known through mythical names or names suggesting innocence such as "Cupidon," "Colombe," or "Rosette." Their onomastic indicates their victimhood.

What's more, the loss of identity becomes the preamble for the months'-long debauch. On the eve of the ordeal, the Duc of Blangis assembles the company and announces:

You are outside France, deep in an uninhabited forest, beyond the highest mountains where the roads were destroyed as soon as you passed over them. You are locked in an impenetrable castle; no one knows you're here. You are taken away from your friends, your parents, you are already dead to the world, and you now only live and breathe for our pleasure.[29]

As if to assure the assembly of their lack of status he continues, "Realize that we don't see you as humans but only as animals that one feeds in the hopes of getting them to work and that one dashes with blows when service is refused."[30] The castle itself becomes the place of anonymity, where identities are erased. All ties are severed: figuratively as with family ties, but literally as well as when the roads are made impassable to prevent escape. Although the preamble of *The 120 Days of Sodom* lists the players in the castle ordeal, many of the names function as pseudonyms, erasing identity and substituting it with a description of roles within the sexual economy of the castle. The use value of human life has reduced the victims to animals, merely surviving at the bidding of higher beings. In a way, this loss of identity prepares the terrain for the staging of sexuality and of a veritable theatrical production, as we shall see in the next chapter.

In the four friends—the Duc of Blangis, President Curval, Durcet, and the Bishop of ***—we see the supreme triumph of the nobility overpowering society. In them we see that Sade brought Enlightenment critique of society to the extreme and reveals its weakness. Giovanni Dall'Orto reminds us, "Having reached this point of no return, libertine thought could only be condemned to extinction. In the end, the French Revolution destroyed once and for all the aristocratic social fabric that held libertinism's few remaining threads."[31] Sade's texts seem to suggest triumph, but perhaps it is the last gasp of a society at the end.

Sade's life and works foretell his age. By relentlessly pursuing and writing about multiple ways of forming and expressing sexual identity, Sade contributed to the polysemic possibilities of identity. The use of sodomy as a metaphor for the rejection of all values and systems is not new with Sade. If one looks at a seventeenth-century text such as *Le Parasite mormon* (*The Mormon Parasite*), its protagonist is accused of sodomy, though later acquitted. This comic novel, said to be written by Charles Sorel and some of his contemporaries, satirizes every literary convention and every trope imaginable. The accusation of sodomy that opens the book clearly situates the work as an act of heresy. Thus, Sade was in many ways picking up on an established strategy for subverting the order and for returning chaos and unpredictability to rational discourse.

## WRITING TO THE END

This subheading is one of the last lines in one of Hervé Guibert's last texts, *Cytomégalovirus: Journal d'Hospitalisation* (*Cytomegalovirus: A Hospitalization Diary*). Terrified of losing his sight to the virus attacking his weakened immune system, Guibert is most worried about losing the ability to write. He clings to the stub of a pencil he's been able to hide from the nursing staff as he waits in the hospital. Writing, like the IV line in his arm, is the only life support left to him. Writing was for Guibert his life, and his life was what he wrote about. He often dissected his family, showing the ugly and the curious as well as the beautiful, perhaps as a way to show and cure the disease he felt in them. He also wrote of friends and lovers who came into his life at various times. His lovers knew his body when it was well, and his texts often have the healthy male body engaged in sexuality as their center. His narrative follows the trajectory of his body in some ways. Sexuality is part of the narrative when the body is well; decay becomes the centerfold when the body is dying. Like Sade, in Guibert, the body described in a transgressive way becomes the center of his texts.

Guibert rebelled against his bourgeois upbringing and wrote savagely of his parents in many of his texts. He was born in 1955 in Paris, but his middle-class family moved soon after to La Rochelle on the Atlantic coast. Guibert seemed to despise his family, except for two great-aunts, Suzanne and Louise, sisters ten years apart in age. Guibert identified with them, as he poignantly mentioned in his late works, in his body. As his body submitted to the viral infection that would kill him, he saw himself decay. As his body withered away, he wrote that he was beginning to resemble the two octo- and nonagenarian aunts physically as well as spiritually.

At the age of twenty, Guibert went to Paris after passing the baccalauréat exam. He tried a career in the theater, working for several companies before beginning work as a journalist and photographer. He never completely abandoned the stage and screen, however. He co-wrote a screenplay *L'Homme blessé* (*The Wounded Man*) with Patrice Chéreau; the film won a César for best screenplay at the Cannes film festival in 1984. He also produced and starred—if I can use that term—in a heartbreakingly revealing film, *La Pudeur ou l'impudeur* (*Modesty or Immodesty*), in which he filmed his body from June 1990 to March 1991 as he was dying of AIDS, focusing the camera on his dying body, his attempt at suicide, and his musings on life. When Guibert died, French national networks decided to air the film, but at the last minute, they changed its time slot from a prime-time to late-night showing.[32]

Guibert's employment as a journalist coincided with his budding career as a photographer when he became the photography critic for *Le Monde*. In 1981, his first collection of short stories appeared, and he produced twenty-eight works in total.[33]

His works can in some regards be divided into two periods: before and after AIDS.[34] Several texts and both compilations of photographs before he was diagnosed with AIDS are complex semiautobiographical accounts of gay sexuality in which the act of writing, the sexual act, and the act of viewing are intertwined. These earlier texts allude to sickness, friends with mysterious illness, and even some overt references to AIDS, but disease is not the primary focus of these texts. For Caron, in Guibert's *A l'ami qui ne m'a pas sauvé la vie* (*To the Friend Who Did Not Save My Life*), AIDS seems to have given Guibert's work/autobiography its final cohesion. Guibert had always been obsessed with the dissolution of the body, especially his own, and AIDS ironically and tragically gave him the opportunity to explore the theme to its full extent.[35]

Several early texts present savage critiques of family, of lineage, and of biography, and Guibert unflinchingly penetrates the small bourgeois mentality he perceived in his parents. In *Mes parents* (*My Parents*), for example, the most autobiographical approach possible turns the genre of biography on its head. This text presents itself as an autobiography, but Guibert focuses instead on describing his parents: their faults, flaws, unrequited desires, and

small mentalities. Although biography and, to an extent, autobiography are expected to unmask and unveil, not only praise, its
subject, Guibert's portrayal of his parents shows them as insignificant, small, and cruel. His biography, therefore, already contains within it the seeds of the perversions he will explore. As is
the case with a later text, *Vice,* Guibert notes true perversion in
the smallest details, in the proper manners and forms performed
to excess, so dear to the petite bourgeoisie from whence he
came.[36] In *My Parents,* Guibert tells us that the biography is always elusive. The figure of Guibert's mother comes into focus
most of all in an early chapter as a simple, mindless, but at times
desperately loved woman in Guibert's life. In the text, he has his
mother pose for a photo, and she takes joy in getting ready for it,
dressing up. However, due to technical problems, the photo of
the mother that he took comes up blank. Guibert reflects that it
is as though his mother, who came alive in preparation for the
photo, had in fact disappeared.[37] Guibert notes an almost impossible lineage between himself and his mother. Guibert relates the
photo unmade to his mother's refusal to tell her son details of
her life. He has no parents, no lineage from which he came.

In this text, there is also a false biography of Guibert's Aunt Suzanne. His two great-aunts, Suzanne and Louise, constitute a leit-
motif of Guibert's work. They are a part of his biography he
acknowledges and cherishes to some extent, bringing them back
into his texts at several points in his career.[38] These two older
women become increasingly important to him as his own body
dies. He watches his body age, and the bodies of these older relatives become models for his own. He sees himself in them more
than he did in his parents. This transferal of connection translates
into fragmented discourse. In a review of this work in *Libération,*
Antoine de Gaudemar says Guibert's writing is "fragmented, as
though constantly surprised by itself, searching for its breath, ob-
stinately refusing all lyrical deportment."[39] For Guibert, problema-
tizing identity decenters language.

Absence of biography—losing oneself in the crowd—becomes
the central metaphor of another text from the middle period,
*L'Incognito.* This work relates a biographical incident at the Aca-
démie Espagnole (Elba). It contains a subtext of Rome, the city
with many identities, a city of layers and historical complexity.
This is also the first text where AIDS becomes a subtext. The title

of the text, *Incognito*, refers to one of the bars of Rome. Here, the biography fades as the lack of identity comes to the foreground of the text. Illness has a way of muting identity: The narrator understands a mysterious illness circulating among friends, acquaintances, and anonymous contacts only as a way to have an identity. Hiding, being incognito, becomes almost impossible when one's identity is marked by disease.

One of Guibert's most important techniques comes to the fore here: the use of false narrative creating a false biography. Denying identity and having fiction mask reality or masquerade as reality as it did in certain eighteenth-century texts plays a role in Guibert. Blanckeman reminds us, "Several novels of the eighteenth century in their preface already identified themselves as fiction that is as doubling, and announced themselves as 'real' texts miraculously found in some attic, at the bottom of the fateful trunk . . . .thus, writing opens up to reality and tries to collect its living scraps."[40] Similarly, Guibert relies on strategies of genres such as biography and autobiography to lead the reader off the track. He provides just enough detail the reader can identify as part of Guibert's biography—a writer dying of AIDS, famous people whom one can identify, family members that existed—to lead us to read his text as though the narrator were only Guibert. At this point, as we shall see, Guibert often introduces a disturbing element—pedophilia or murder—to make us doubt the narrator's identity.

As could be said of Sade's works, dissimulation passing for reality is not only the true nature of literature, but a strategy for multiplying identities. In Guibert's early works as well as texts written once he was dying, the texts play with reality as a way to control, perhaps hang onto, identity. When he was diagnosed with AIDS in 1988, his works began to confront the disease and the disease in him head on. Some of his most famous works—*To the Friend Who Did Not Save My Life, The Compassion Protocol, L'Homme au chapeau rouge (The Man with the Red Hat),* and *Cytomegalovirus: A Hospitalization Diary*—all deal with coming to terms with terminal disease, attempts at experimental treatments, the search for cures not yet readily available legally, and facing the prospect of blindness because of cytomegalovirus, with the impending impossibility of continuing to write. The pen and the IV line are both lifelines in the hospital as he waits for a cure. *The Man in the Red Hat* was written in early 1991, followed in summer of that year by *Paradise,* then in fall by *Cytomegalovirus: A Hospitalization Diary,* the diary of his hospitalization. The latter two were to be published posthumously.

Guibert's literary popularity skyrocketed when he appeared on the French program *Apostrophes* on March 16, 1990, to discuss *To the Friend Who Did Not Save My Life.*[41] This enormously popular weekly program hosted by Bernard Pivot brought literary figures to television to discuss their works. On the program, Guibert discussed his illness very openly. Pivot had organized the program around the theme "homicidal sexuality," with several guests including Guibert, a psychologist, and a journalist. Of the group, Guibert ended up being cast as "the victim," the one who had been invited to discuss his disease as he lived it. Pivot asked Guibert on the air about his declaration that he would commit suicide. The program produced an outpouring of sympathy and was one of the highest rated ever. Guibert's frank and poignant testimonial of his disease on national television also brought AIDS awareness into French consciousness as no political discourse had been able to do until then.[42]

Guibert's reputation was also enhanced, perhaps some would say tarnished, by his reputed liaisons with some of the most influential men of letters in France, such as Roland Barthes. For his barely veiled references to Michel Foucault—Muzil in several of his works—the press chastised Guibert. Foucault died in 1984, but the French media scrupulously respected his wishes by not revealing the cause of his death as AIDS. French newspaper obituaries at the time listed the cause of death as cancer. With Guibert's veiled reference to Foucault in his own work, however, some friends of the historian felt Guibert was revealing too much about him in a way Foucault would not have wanted. A Foucault-like character appears in a short story "Les Secrets d'un homme" ("Secrets of a Man") and in *To the Friend Who Did Not Save My Life,* among other texts. In this text, Guibert/the narrator traces the illness and death of Muzil, and this gives the impetus to the "history of AIDS" as the narrator lived it. He notes the line of his friends and lovers who have become ill and died before him as a way of creating a biography for his illness. To this day, along with Cyril Collard, the author of the novel *Les Nuits fauves* (*Savage*

*Nights*),[43] Guibert remains one of the best-known writers of AIDS
novels in France.

Guibert's sexual identity clearly defines from the outset his
identity as human being and as writer. Creating autofictions
about gay sexuality means recreating his own biography—
sometimes viewing it through distorting lenses, but revealing it
clearly through others. This does not, however, make Guibert a
gay writer as we sometimes understand the term, especially in
the United States. He does not write about gay sexuality as a way
to politicize sexuality or as a way to confront heterosexual he-
gemony. Guibert is not a militant gay writer, using his craft to
create a less hostile environment for gays. Derek Duncan, for example, looks at Guibert within the context of gay literature and
sees that he identifies more with a coterie of Parisian elites than
he does with a gay culture.[44]

Instead, Guibert takes for granted, in some sense, that sexual
identity means desiring bodies of the same sex. Perhaps that is
why he describes the body's sexuality in rational terms. He has
gone beyond the dichotomies between sexuality and rationality.
His identity is the gay body, and he expressed it in his writings.
The disease that killed him also became a marker of a new phase
of bodily identity: the gay young-old man confronting death.

## Works Both Barbarous and Delicate

Guibert himself noted an affinity between his work and that of
Sade based on this principle of delicacy. As we have seen, "le fameux principe de délicatesse" that Guibert noted in his novel
gathers inspiration from Sade's November 23–24, 1783, letter
from prison in which he refers to délicatesse. Sade here defines
his approach to debauchery as the contrast between things bizarre and delicate, establishing a polarity that Guibert clearly
found intriguing in all its subversive pleasures. That Guibert defines this principle as *fameux* may allude to Barthes's *Sade, Fourier, Loyola,* where this citation forms the basis of Barthes's
reflection.

Part of the reason Sade inspired Guibert lies in Sade's influence
on French letters in general. Sade's reputation was based on
hearsay and on his texts, although his works had an uneven dis-

tribution during his lifetime. *The 120 Days of Sodom* was not published until 1904; the manuscript was taken from the Bastille and
circulated in private hands for almost 150 years. *Justine* was published during his lifetime, but, while enormously popular, it did
not generate great revenue for the marquis. His political tracts
written during the Revolution were published; yet they did not
advance his reputation as a novelist, but rather as a philosophe
and, ironically for a member of one of the most unrepentant feu-
dal aristocratic families left in France by the end of the eighteenth century, a revolutionary. *Justine* continued to circulate
throughout the nineteenth century, but Sade's reputation waned.
His writings became somewhat influential again as inspiration
for Baudelaire's satanic texts. Still, Sade's works themselves remained in the "hell" of the Bibliothèque Nationale in Paris for
the most part until the beginning of the twentieth century, when
the poet Apollinaire rediscovered several of them. Apollinaire
published selected pages in 1909.

Then, the psychiatrist Maurice Heine published several other
texts between 1926 and 1935 and thus begins the real, primary
influence of Sade in the twentieth century. The surrealists name
him one of their own. André Breton's *Premier manifeste du surréa-
lisme (First Surrealist Manifesto)* lists several precursors of surrealism, and Sade is listed as a "surrealist because of his sadism."[45]
The surrealist film *Âge d'or (Age of Gold)*, co-directed and written
by Luis Buñuel and Salvador Dalí, makes explicit reference to the
final scenes of *The 120 Days of Sodom* in which the Duc of Blangis
and the other remaining survivors of the 120 days of torture in
the castle of Silling surface from the ruins. In a typical surrealist
twist, the last scene shows the Duc crucified, thus mixing sacred
and profane elements so as to shock bourgeois audiences. Authors and movements in the twentieth century appropriated the
transgressive nature of Sade's ideas. In fact, as I noted in the introduction, tackling the figure of Sade and coming to terms with
what Sade the man, the writer, and the reprobate meant and
could mean for the twentieth century became in some sense a
rite of passage for post-1945 intellectuals in France. Being able to
write about Sade, about perhaps the most contradictory of figures—at once reactionary aristocrat and revolutionary, at once
family man and depraved libertine, at once philosophe and philosopher of evil—meant being able to tackle one of the most

complex literary images possible. Just as the marquis constantly tested the limits of society, laws, and morality, studying the marquis has become a test of one's intellectual flexibility. He was forbidden fruit, thus irresistible.[46]

In his texts, Guibert hides behind names, often alluding to presumably real persons in his fiction by an initial or an assumed name. The narrator of Guibert's text also hides, only occasionally flirting with the reader by naming himself "G," "HG," or even "Hervé." Clearly the reader is to make some connection between the narrator and the author, but then the text recounts a sexual encounter with such force or of such deviance that the reader refuses to make the connection. As with Sade, the life of the author becomes confused with the life of the fictional characters, and each feeds off the reputation of the other. The autobiography becomes problematic in Guibert, as it certainly was for Sade. In one way, Guibert revealed himself over and over again to us through numerous photographic self-portraits. At times, he stares at the viewer through an unfocused lens, at others, he peers at the mirror or out a window, bringing only a reflection back to us. More provocative are portraits and self-portraits of body parts, such as hands and feet, where bodies are fragmented before the camera. Again, although ostensibly revealing himself to the viewer, Guibert's photographs conceal as they reveal.

In Guibert's texts, especially his later ones, hiding the identities of those he knows who have died of AIDS becomes one of the most preposterous erasures of the text—preposterous precisely because the references were so thinly veiled that Guibert was accused of revealing information that his friends would have instead wanted hidden. In *The Man in the Red Hat,* Guibert/the narrator talks of the continuing process of illness, of AIDS, through the traces left on his body: the throat spots, for example. The narrator talks of paintings: real ones versus forgeries. Searching for "the real thing" recalls the search for self-identity when surrounded by the potential for false identity. The text culminates with a lost manuscript, an unfinished text and an unfinishable book, and the prospect of never having the time to start again. In *To the Friend Who Did Not Save My Life,* the narrator notes that AIDS is for him, "my paradigm in my project to self-revelation."[47] Writing is the only true revelation of the self. Biography does not exist as such because texts are the real remnants of the body, of the person succumbing to disease.

Although Guibert's interest in Sade may be partially tributary of this larger intellectual symbolism of Sade as subject par excellence of French intellectual letters, in studying Guibert's works, certain points of convergence and of philosophical rapprochement between Sade's ideas and Guibert's emerge. Sade's real biography became entwined with and enhanced by his text. For Buot, "His will to shuffle the deck shows itself also in the stories he writes: the interest in incognito, pseudonyms, and other reinventions of the self represents an attempt to let go of a too-limited identity. Hervé practices the truncated autobiography, the diary, but the principal character is fictional."[48] Physical bodies are the manifestations of identity, and components of the body's relationship with its surroundings add to the sense of self. Sexual identity, creating a link with others through the body, is at the core of a sense of identity for Guibert, and it was for Sade as well. Both authors, however, problematize identity and begin to decouple the link between the body and the self.

# 2

# Sexual Performance: Staging and Watching Bodies in the Act

IDENTITY CAN BE CREATED, DENIED, AND DISTORTED FOR PERSONAL OR LIT-erary ends. In Sade and Guibert, the self shifts shapes in both bio-graphical and fictional accounts. Sexuality, part of what forms the body's identity, comes into play within the context of self-awareness. Guibert makes sexuality, the body's contours in the same-sex act, an indelible part of his characters' characteristics. Hiding one's identity also can mean hiding sexuality, practicing sex in the shadows, and nameless and faceless sex. Sexual iden-tity at other times asserts itself in his narrator, reveling in the in-tricacies of this same sex act that confers meaning and identity on the narrator and his lovers. Sexual identity needs to go public if it is to become a marker of identity in Guibert. Sexuality acts; the theatricality of sex reveals and affirms identity.

To turn this assertion around, sexuality can be staged and often is. Recreating the physical reality of the theater and sharing on stage an act usually considered intimate and private allows sexu-ality to become a key fact of identity formation. For Guibert, sex often takes place as though on stage, with many theatrical ele-ments present. In this, once again Sade becomes a precursor. For Sade, sexual acts are public spectacles.

In both Sade and Guibert, theatricality is literal. Sade wrote plays and created an elaborate theater in his Provençal château where he had many of them staged. For an iconoclast such as Sade, however, "The very conventionality of the plays is interest-ing," explains Julie Chandler Hayes. "The plays are beset with an overwhelming alterity, haunted by the presence of other writers, imaginary audiences, both real and supposed critics; they be-speak a slavish devotion to theatrical conventions and norms."[1] Sade also acted and directed plays in the theater of the asylum where he spent his last years, a venue created as an outlet for inmates' aggression. Sade's theatrical works, however, are not very well known, perhaps because they seem less provocative than his prose works. Sade's reputation is built on the lengthy novels he wrote mostly in prison. Even his nontheatrical texts are filled with theatrical spaces, however. For example, Barthes, in *Sade, Fourier, Loyola,* describes Sade's fictional castle in *The 120 Days of Sodom,* "The principal site at the Château de Silling is the theater of debauchery where everyone meets daily from 5 to 10 p.m. In this theater, everyone is actor and spectator. The area is therefore simultaneously that of a *mimesis,* here purely auditory, consigned to the storyteller's narrative, and of *praxis* (a conjunction attempted, generally unsuccessfully, by many avant-garde theaters)."[2] Theaters or theatrical spaces provide stages for sexual display in Sade's works because the theater allows him to bring his provocation to the public.

In a gesture similar to that of the autobiography that affirms and denies identity and the body, a theme explored in the previous chapter, bringing the body to a stage for performance distances the body from its identity. Autobiography should bring the author, whole, to the attention of the viewer. Guibert, and often Sade, however, do not allow this reappropriation by the viewer. The details of their lives do not form biographies, that is, coherent narratives of the past to elucidate the present and anticipate the future; instead, they form an essential hide-and-seek with the reader. Insistence on playing out sexuality for an audience, and bringing the body's most intimate reality into the public space does the same. The private body is thrust toward the viewer, the voyeur, but still partially hidden from view because of an overlay of rationality in place of the raw emotional depth usually associated with sexuality.

One of the main points of convergence between the works of the two authors is their desire to unmask sexuality, literally stripping the theatrical mask from the sexual self. Human propensity for creating a social self through adopting masks was articulated to great effect in Erving Goffman's classic and still useful study *The Presentation of Self in Everyday Life.* For Goffman, the mask is "our truer self, the self we would like to be."[3] In all public situations, we adopt masks as a means of assuming different selves.

Goffman's *Stigma* continues his work on the social construction of identity begun in *The Presentation of Self in Everyday Life.* The earlier text had proposed the idea that construction of self shifts with social situations. Identity, like a mask, can be both changing and multiple for any one body. In *Stigma,* he explores the selves that are somehow damaged in terms of social identity through a variety of factors ranging from physical deformities to "outcast" religious affiliations. These "stigmata" negotiated, denied, defiantly proclaimed, hidden, and expunged depend on the circumstances. One of Goffman's stigmata is the designation "homosexual." We recall that even according to Butler, gender and sexuality are cultural constructs. Gender becomes not a biological given, but a social construct, a mask, and a persona. For Guibert, the stigma of homosexuality is often defiantly proclaimed, but he acquires the stigma of disease that forces him to again alter his social identity. Self-identity, damaged identity, and the various social roles stigma plays remain key to understanding Guibert.

Goffman dedicates the last section of his work to derivations and deviance. In terms of identity construction, *deviance* is defined relative to a group expectation of behavior. Individuals who deviate from a norm but remain within groups of stigmatized individuals with shared behaviors or beliefs are "socially deviant" where a band of like-acting deviants decline their social roles. Individuals who move away from the group are considered "eccentrics."[4]

An important aspect of Goffman's work is an elaboration of a theory of "passing," moving between groups in an effort to seek acceptance. Goffman sees passing as an action often falling between extremes "of complete secrecy on one hand and complete information on the other, it would seem that the problems people face who make a concerted and well-organized effort to pass are problems that wide ranges of persons face at some time or other."[5] Those who attempt to pass go through a cycle, moving from unwitting passing, to intentional, to passing "for fun," and so on, until a potential "disappearance" that may be as extreme as passing in all situations so as to completely adopt the assumed identity, and even moving to another city to begin again.[6] Similarly, Eve Kosofsky Sedgwick explores passing as a nonstructured binary, not just an action taking place between knowing and unknowing subjects.[7] For Goffman, there exists a world for those without stigmata and one for those with stigmata, and passing allows negotiation between the two. Passing itself is a complex act, where various phases or steps and degrees of acceptance are possible. For Sedgwick, the boundaries themselves between categories, between the "well" and the "afflicted," are less rigid, allowing passing to take place in a more structured, less linear way.

These studies of human behavior and group interaction can explain the intricate connection in both Sade and Guibert between concealing identities and revealing new ones in a public forum. Adopting masks is one human response to the need to integrate into a variety of social settings; passing is a common response of the stigmatized to being excluded, for it affords the possibility of acceptance. Moving between two groups—those with and without stigma—or even discovering that there are more than two groups—that "the closet" is not an entirely hermetic space—resonates in the works of Sade and Guibert. Sade's iconoclasm and his descriptions of extreme behavior pushed at the rigid walls of Enlightenment rational discourse. Guibert's narrators in his autofictions assume various personas as they adopt or reject various sexual selves.

If adopting a sexual mask, a sexual identity, is part of our social masquerade, both Sade and Guibert point to the mask before they reveal the identity underneath. According to C. S. Peirce, indexical signs point to their referent. For Guibert and Sade, the sex act is not a way to hide identity or to conceal oneself, but rather it is a way to be tethered to the dissection table ready for autopsy, ready to reveal all. In these two authors, sexuality becomes a form of defiance. It also by necessity must become part of an exteriorization of the self for the consumption of others. In this way, it resembles the theater, where masks, disguises, and interchangeable personae consume the "reality" of the presentation and substitute for it. In *Sexual Personae. Art and Decadence from Nefertiti to Emily Dickinson,* Camille Paglia states, "The theatricality of Sade's libertines comes from their clarity of consciousness. Daydreaming or introspection is unneeded in a world where realization immediately follows desire. The libertines are like Roman emperors in wealth and power, two things, as Sade observes, which give absolute sexual control over others."[8] Guibert's texts, too, bring clarity of consciousness into the sexual arena. In this chapter, we shall explore how identity and sexuality are concealed and revealed.

## STAGING BODIES

In her study of Sade's theatrical production, Hayes concludes, "His approach can be seen in many respects as a subversion of bourgeois drama. It seems clear from a look at those plays which Sade himself classed as dramas that what counted in his eyes were either the trappings of the so-called *drame anglais*—murders, imprisonments, poison, and even ghosts—or the titillating family entanglements of the French *genre sérieux*."[9] Sade always considered himself a man of the theater, but for Hayes, his plays are not entirely satisfying. The idea of theater for Sade was not that of a space for radical experimentation. Although his texts did, as Hayes says, subvert "bourgeois drama," they are nonetheless inscribed within a conventional framework. Sade's literal forays into the theater seem, therefore, somewhat disappointing by their conventionality.

More important perhaps for our purposes, the theater was, for Sade, a metaphorical space where the private could be rendered public. In his biography of Sade, Lever traces Sade's fascination with theater rather than theatrical production. The subsequent mutation of this interest into a theatricalization of sex began in Sade's formative years. "Theatricality, flagellation, sodomy, passivity: all the themes that make up Sadeian eroticism were thus potentially combined in his actual or fantasized experience at Louis-le Grand," the prestigious high school Sade attended.[10] The connection between the two is almost existential, notes Annie Le Brun. "For Sade too, nature is seen as the only theatre of activity; but a theatre whose every element may suddenly assume a decisive importance in the drama being played."[11] Sade saw the theater as a possible framework for existence. It is, however, the idea of the theater as an ensemble of elements that allows the public access to private interactions that concerns us most in this discussion. If the theater provides a stage for action, then rendering the sexual act public theatricalizes it. Sade brings elements of the theater into all his genres. Didier Derson even notes specific theatrical conventions such as *monologue, récit, didascalie,* and *ti-*

*rade* (taken from theories of classical theater) in Sade's novels.[12] So to understand the scope of Sade's interest in theater, we must look less to Sade's theatrical production per se to understand what theater meant to him. It seems theater is a metaphor for a way of approaching identity, of bringing the body into contact with its surroundings. The body in all its dimensions becomes spectacle, ritual, ceremony, and display. Octavio Paz notes that for Sade, "The erotic ceremony turns into a philosophical ballet and a mathematical sacrifice. A theater not of characters but of situations, or more exactly, demonstrations. A ritual theater that works both the mystery plays of Calderón and the human sacrifices of the Aztecs, possessed by the same geometric furor."[13]

We shall return to the geometric obsession in Sade, for what links Sade to the Enlightenment thinkers is not only his exploration of the limits of reason as an abstract concept. Sade's texts cast their discussion of the limits of acceptable discourse in terms that are highly precise and geometrical. Calculations and numerical combinations abound. Of particular interest here is Paz's statement that Sade's sexual description belies empiricism typical of the expository modes of his age, that is, the need to demonstrate what is hypothesized. And, lastly, Paz's idea of Sade's sexual display as ceremony seems particularly useful. Not only is sexuality public, but it is openly acted out in such a way as to confer on it a ceremonial aura.

Sex is staged in a theatrical space in Sade's texts. For the discussions that follow, Sade's *120 Days of Sodom* comes to mind, although many of his texts could provide material for analysis. As the narrator of *The 120 Days of Sodom* describes Durcet's castle at Silling, site of the group's depraved rituals, the rooms are depicted as having been arranged specifically to facilitate the months'-long orgies. Of particular interest is the assembly room, destined for the historians' narratives, the battlefield of the projected combats.[14] The semicircular room has a throne at one end, on the stage, destined for the narrator. The room's configuration is such that the audience would be able to hear every word because the narrator is placed as in an actor's theater.[15] The room is filled with props and instruments of torture used to punish transgressions. The entire production of sexuality takes place in a theatrical space.

In Sade, sex is theater also through excessive performance.

Sexuality is public and almost always presumes an explicit audience. We could say, along with Alan Corkhill, "To a large extent the aggressively phallocentric libertines populating Sade's clandestine narratives—drawn as they are from across the social ranks—are lonely nihilists who engage in games of exhibitionism and voyeurism in semi-public arenas, thereby flouting the Enlightenment principle of the right to privacy and personal intimacy."[16] The orgy is one of the most common forms of sexual display in Sade's works. In *Justine,* characters are raped in secluded areas, but sex acts performed in groups dominate the text. Performance is also emphasized by rigid orchestration of the sex act. The aggressors and their victims are expected to perform on command, at prescribed times, and in preordained ways, eliminating all spontaneity. Also, in Sade's world, size matters, with measurements of genitalia and the prowess of aggressors being highlighted numerous times in the texts. The sexual act is also often dependent on props of all kinds in the torture chambers and the bedrooms. In *The 120 Days of Sodom,* several "new inventions" appear, such as whipping machines to which the victims are hooked for easier administration of punishment for minor infractions of the strict order of the castle, impregnating machines, raping machines, and orgasm machines, all of which enhance the sexual act. In the case of the latter three machines, their introduction into the routine heralds a new phase of existence at Silling Castle. Since the human body no longer suffices, since sexuality in all of its possibilities has been exhausted, machines begin to take over where the "mere body" once sufficed.

Most important, perhaps, if sex takes place onstage in front of others, those others assume a role as silent witnesses, as voyeurs. Those who read the text or see the play, of course, always assume the role of voyeur, witnessing a story played before their eyes without participating. The orgy provides a somewhat intermediate space for the voyeur in that, often, and depending on the context, the voyeurs may be called on or allowed to enter as participants. Moving from the passive to the active role—shifting identity—allows for adoption of multiple selves within the same spaces. Theatricalizing sexuality, rendering it public, and moving it from a private to a public activity allow the actors and spectators to assume different selves in the process as well.

The orgy has particular importance in Sade as a theatrical ges-

ture, and the illustrations to several of his texts help us understand the intricate nature of its construction. Not all Sade's texts
included illustrations. Of those that did, *Aline et Valcour* showed
fourteen engravings in its first edition; the second contained sixteen. All are unsigned. Delon notes, "The totality of the illustrations tells, with obsessive insistence, of threats against the female
body: beaten, thrown into a tomb, stripped and palpated, lust-
fully manhandled, stabbed, stripped and tortured, decapitated,
lying stabbed."[17] The first edition of *Justine,* supervised by Sade,
included a frontispiece signed Philippe Chery but without the
name of the author. Subsequent editions added illustrations. *La
nouvelle Justine ou les malheurs de la vertu (The New Justine or
the Misfortunes of Virtue)* and *L'Histoire de Juliette (The Story of
Juliette)* were published with ten unsigned illustrations per volume for a total of one hundred illustrations. These engravings
privilege scenes of couplings of all kinds with genitalia fully visible. Some texts such as *Philosophy in the Boudoir* provided only
frontispieces, often allegorical in nature.

    In all cases, as Delon notes, "Sade and his book sellers know
the importance of images in pornographic literature."[18] Seduction and arousal often depend on and certainly are enhanced by
visual stimulation to illustrate the textual details. Although Sade's
texts describe the human configurations we are exploring here,
the textual illustrations provide clarification of the metaphorical
implications of these constructions made from human bodies.
Sade's orgies always involve switching roles, according to Kathryn Norberg, and that explains to some extent the preference for
sodomy since anyone can play the passive role. Gender becomes
less important as a category in a sexual relationship not of man-
woman, man-man, woman-woman, but of master-slave.[19] Delon
explains the inclusion of illustrations in *The New Justine,* for
example, as a part of the process of amplification the text under-
went through its various revisions. The shortish text *Les Infor-
tunes de la vertu (The Misfortunes of Virtue)* was notably
expanded and somewhat modified to become *Justine.* The suc-
cess of the latter led to publication of *The New Justine,* again a
substantially expanded version with respect to its predecessor.
Between *Justine* and *The New Justine,* at least four etchings were
added that "gave to certain scenes the evidence of the phan-
tasm."[20]

In the illustrations to several of Sade's texts, the nature of the forms created as humans couple with one another seems not only implausible but also highly stylized. The orgy here is not the chaotic melee of Federico Fellini's *Satyricon* or Michelangelo Antonioni's *Zabriskie Point*,[21] two films that include scenes of couplings between groups of people. In these two films, the orgy is the moment of abandon, and that spontaneity is mirrored in the unstructured masses of bodies. The orgy represents visually the moment of confusion when the spectator is not able to see the forms in front of him/her clearly. The orgy, therefore, would be a moment of freedom in the film; sexuality presents the possibility of liberation. In *Zabriskie Point*, in fact, the orgy takes place in the desert locale that gives its name to the film; sexuality is a force of nature, celebrated in public.

In Sade's texts, with their emphasis on enclosure and imprisonment, where the sexual act is performed on victims chosen against their will for their physical attributes, we are not surprised that the sexuality of the text is constrained. In certain illustrations, the characters are literally "trussed up" for sex, bound, and awaiting their turn. In this sense, freedom is the antithesis of sexuality. Also in these drawings, the systems of ropes and pulleys on which the victims hang are reminiscent of the structures behind the scenes in the theater. The body here does not know the abandon of sexual gratification. Instead, it is harnessed for show and for the gratification of the four friends, but perhaps, in the theatrical metaphor, also for the voyeur/spectator.

In other illustrations, we see another side of the theatricality of sex in Sade. They depict orgy scenes of bodies piled high in human pyramids of couplings. These ensembles are reminiscent of daredevil acts or the high-wire act at the circus. The "thrills" of defying gravity that the spectator feels watching these acts are tempered by the knowledge that one false move will topple the group. So here, too, freedom and spontaneity are completely absent from the sex act. Instead, Sade groups his bodies like an architectural project or an inanimate space on which the four friends can satisfy their libertine desires.

Guibert joins the performance of gender and identity to the elements that Sade had already proposed to create a theatrical space for sexuality. In Guibert's texts, gay sexuality becomes an identity among many, displayed at crucial moments and down-played at others. Theatrical couplings, orgies, and suggestions of pedophilia lead to an unmasking of conventional sexuality that points in an indexical way to the mask behind which sexuality usually remains hidden. The protection of an explicit sexual persona allows Guibert to assume different sexual guises.[22] At times, however, the mask falls. Exposing the body or lifting the veil becomes a theatrical gesture in Guibert. (In the film *La Pudeur ou l'impudeur*, for example, Guibert exposes his own body dying of AIDS as his voice-over unmasks the physical realities of the body with AIDS for the viewer.) Guibert unmasks gay sexuality to expose the scenery behind the curtain.

In an early text, *La Mort propagande*, Guibert casts the text itself as theater. "My body, whether under the effects of orgasm, or under the effect of sorrow, is in a state of theatricality, of paroxysm, that I must reproduce somehow, whether in a photo, on film, or on a tape."[23] Guibert understands the body as the locus of an exterior gaze, where it becomes the stage for the voyeur's *jouissance*. But Guibert also thwarts the power of that gaze by making his own gaze the only one that counts. He will be the one to film, to photograph, to control the camera, and to tape. In this way, the body that would have been given up for exposure is in fact the locus of a defiant gaze toward the spectator. This defiance seems reminiscent of Frida Kahlo's self-portraits that depict her staring straight at the viewer; the voyeur comes to pry into her physical pain.[24] These intruders cause pain because they remain outside in the wings, judging from a privileged distance.

In this delineated space inside and outside the closet, on stage, or in the seats, movement between zones occurs. For Sade, orgies allow participants to change roles. The orgy provides a bridge, a fluid zone, where those outside can come inside the action. This, however, destroys the illusion of intimacy of the act; the theatrical "third wall" no longer exists. For Guibert, the body itself can be the stage where the audience members fix their gaze. As the body changes, as it becomes diseased, the identity—the mask—changes with it. The body itself mediates between inside and outside as a way to assume a shifting identity. The intimacy of the sexual act is denied in both Sade and Guibert.

VOYEURS, ACTORS, AND THEATRICAL IDENTITY

Guibert's texts present the reader with scenes of group sex, certainly calculated to shock the sensibilities of the despised petite
bourgeoisie. But Guibert does not intend his works to amount
merely to their shock value. These scenes of public sex acts continue an exploration of sexuality as a manifestation of identity.
Sexuality's shifting parameters contribute to multiple identities
and to the many ways in which identities can be hidden or modified.

Like Sade, Guibert's literary production includes plays, as well
as a film scenario. Guibert wrote three plays: a very early work,
*La Pièce d'Oedipe* (*The Oedipus Play*) (1972) in the collection *La
Mort propagande; Suzanne et Louise* (1977); and *Vole mon
dragon*, published posthumously in 1994. He also co-wrote a film
scenario with Patrice Chéreau, *L'Homme blessé* (*The Wounded
Man*).

In these theatrical texts, Guibert explored the relationship of
love and cruelty, loneliness and yearning for love. In the notes
following the text of *L'Homme blessé*, Chéreau describes the essence of their collaborative film as "absence and treason, what
is normal and what isn't, love at first sight as the beginning of
heartbreak."[25] The themes developed in his novels reverberate in
his theatrical texts as well. But, like Sade, we cannot define Guibert as primarily a playwright. Both authors in some ways be-
lieved themselves to be men of the theater, but their prose texts,
using theatricality as a metaphor, represent their most lasting
contributions.

The text that perhaps most explicitly illustrates Guibert's metaphorical use of the theater as a place to render sexuality public is
*Les Chiens* (The Dogs), a small "plaquette pornographique," in
Guibert's own words, published among his first works. Buot tells
us it is one of Guibert's texts where one finds "sex on every
page."[26] It is a text where "slaves combat in pleasure and violence of all kinds to please a master . . . the ceremony is described
in the smallest detail."[27] As was the case for texts inspired by similar dynamics such as those of Genet and Sade, in *Les Chiens*, a
text of humiliation and degradation, language triumphs. For
Buot, in the text, "All passes through words. Writing is crafted,
there is an extreme joy in speaking about marginal situations, a

willingness to go to the point of no return in laying bare the body, sex, or life itself."[28] *Les Chiens* describes a sexual triangle between two men and a woman. One man, the narrator, remains on the outside watching, the voyeur who cannot participate. When the second man penetrates the woman, however, the voyeur becomes actor, joining into the triangle. In a sense, the narrator must wait for a heterosexual coupling before going public with his own sexuality within this context. The public nature of the sex act in a way allows the narrator to assume his true sexual persona. In *Les Chiens*, Guibert allows his characters to play roles and to assume identities by moving from the space of voyeur to actor.

Looking at oneself from outside through a lens takes on other dimensions in Guibert's work as well. His important work as photographer and filmmaker constantly posits his own body as spectacle. But in ways again reminiscent of Kahlo, the self-portrait often takes on a unexpected defiance. Guibert allows us, the voyeurs, to view his body but not to appropriate it.

In a sense, photography proves to be another metaphor in Guibert's work. This medium (unavailable to Sade) allows for visual reproduction of the various masks of assumed identities, all the while concealing elements as desired. The photograph seems to bear witness to a reality, but as artistic artifact, it also manipulates, poses, and stages reality, all the while freezing it in a pose. Photography allows Guibert to be his own voyeur, in a sense, and project his sense of self onto the Other. The medium allows for a new exploration of the body. Guibert's search for self begins and ends with awareness of the body. His early works from 1977 to 1988 often celebrate the homoerotic body. Guibert's writings after he was diagnosed as HIV-positive in 1988 retain this obsession; they merely refocus on the dying body. The physical effects of disease radically alter the construction of self and Other, a process of erotic doubling omnipresent on a textual level. This process is further complicated by the inclusion of photographs. In fact, photography and the voyeurism inherent in the camera eye are essential components for understanding Guibert's literature. Several of his novels contain photographs that, when accompanying texts, provide a heightened perspective on otherness. For Pascale-Anne Brault, "This indissociable link between the body, the gaze, sexuality and autobiography is exemplified by the fact that Guibert, whose first publications go back to 1977, was also a photography critic for *Le Monde* newspaper from 1977 on." She continues, "Thus body and gaze, text and image are linked, as said in *L'Image fantôme,* in an almost indissociable way, sometimes interchangeably."[29] Eroticism, otherness, and the camera are linked in Guibert's works.

Often for Guibert, the erotic "self" and "Other" merge. The voyeur becomes actor, only to shift positions again in certain texts. The narrator sees himself as an erotic being only through the eyes of the lover. When the self becomes diseased, the doubling becomes tripling; erotic recognition is mediated through the realization of the impossibility of consummation due to disease. This process of doubling and tripling continues in Guibert's photographic novels. The photos in these texts augment, contradict, or double the text. They provide explanation and negate it at the same time, distancing the reader from the text. As in the works of Sade, Guibert's eroticism distances the subject from the object through formal and linguistic techniques. It thus accentuates the split between the self and the Other. For Sade, too, his life was created as double, aristocrat and thinker, the doubling of the self that leads to a doubling of the text. Delon points out the core of the Sadean text is both refined and elitist "in its grammar which organizes the postures, the episodes, the scenes and in the invention of the language capable of saying it."[30] Sadean writing is nourished in the intersection between the crafted syllogism and the exacerbation of a fantasy, between blasphemy and euphemism, crude language and allusion. The work is thus held together by a dynamic of progression of both reading and writing, as well as by a desire that can never be realized.[31] The multiplication of identities—assuming masks and later revealing one or more identities, multiplying selves only to conceal them—provides an essential element of Guibert's texts as it does for Sade. Desire, longing for the Other as mediated through masks, is also inherent in the recognition of photography. An important critical study for understanding the link between photographs, desire, and ultimately death is Barthes's *Camera Lucida.* He writes that photos awaken desire. "This longing to inhabit . . . is fantasmatic, deriving from a kind of second sight which seems to bear me forward to a utopian time, or to carry me back to somewhere in myself."[32] Doubling, desire, and distance mediated

through writing link Guibert and Sade. Doubling of roles—
voyeur, actor, and others—is omnipresent in Guibert's texts,
which often seem autobiographical; the narrative "I" seems to
correspond to the author himself. Yet, there is almost always
something suspect with this "I," making the reader believe that
what seems to be autobiographical is really fiction; Guibert's *je*
(I) is very often *autre* (Other).

In Guibert, doubling often takes the form of the narrator approaching or rejecting an erotic partner. The narrator identifies
and becomes one with the lover, but as disease intervenes in the
relationship, he moves away. Seeing yourself in a body that is
Other but then rejecting it is a show of force. Tracing the erotic
double in Guibert's AIDS text *Fou de Vincent* (*Crazy About Vincent*) from 1988, the narrator/Guibert begins to experience the
disease as Other, through the body of the Other, his diseased
companion, Vincent, a bisexual drug addict. Besides its prominent role in the narrator's erotic encounters, AIDS is also part of
the exoticized Other in this text, particularly as it relates to Africa.
Vincent tells the narrator a story, which revolts him, of an African
restaurant in Paris he frequents where "most of the guys have
AIDS [and] in the kitchen they screw poor, starving girls, without
rubbers, in exchange for a grilled, frozen shark steak."[33] In this
text, the reader witnesses a body that itself is manifesting signs of
the viral Other. In this instance, between the body of the self and
of the Other lies the disease invader. The narrator chronicles his
strange presence truly as though he were a voyeur, watching the
scene from the outside. The erotic relationship is mediated
through the dichotomy between self and Other.

Published in 1990, *To the Friend Who Did Not Save My Life* narrates Guibert's realization that he is infected with AIDS. In this
text, AIDS only exists as its negation, within the boundaries of a
possible cure. Guibert traces the spread of AIDS in his friend,
Muzil (that is, Michel Foucault), in great detail, as though he were
examining the future of his own body in the mirror. Although in
this text the self is diseased, it is still reflected, doubled, through
the suffering of the Other. This novel also presents a sort of "history of AIDS" of those who were "the others" in Guibert's life.
The narrator explains how his lovers discovered they were getting
ill, when he himself first heard of the "gay plague," and when his
friends began to show signs of the disease. In a sense, this per-

sonal chronology of the disease is a way to continue to keep the disease in the realm of the Other. Just as Guibert faces his illness in this novel only from the perspective of a cure, so too does he painstakingly detail the way in which it affected those around him. It is for him an "outline," a structural skeleton for his own work.

Even the cure comes in the form of the Other, of Bill, the mysterious, rich American who promises to enter the narrator in trials of an experimental drug, which he never does. Yet the hope of the cure becomes precisely what the narrator needs to continue writing, which, in the end, is the goal of this last period of his life. For Guibert, AIDS is the paradigm in the project to uncover the self. This novel is an assessment of the illness. AIDS represents a way of structuring the work of writing, which will be the path to uncovering the self. It is through AIDS that the narrator finds a reason to continue to write. Writing, in turn, becomes a way to understand the illness in all its manifestations. The narrator in *Fou de Vincent* surreptitiously came to know the body of his lover and to write about it, to uncover it for himself and for the reader; he undergoes a similar process in *To the Friend Who Did Not Save My Life* with regard to his own body. Guibert's narrative focuses on the body even in his earlier works. His novels written after he contracted AIDS shift from the body of the Other to the body of the self, but the center of observation remains *le corps.*

In 1991, he published *The Compassion Protocol,* in which he narrates his attempts to be included in the trials of another experimental drug. The cures in this book are often described as lethal: several hundred people had died of the DDI "cure" when it was introduced. In this sense, even cures are the negation of healing. The body in this novel may be feeling more alive thanks to new medication, but it is also slipping away from the narrator, becoming the property of a medicalized Other.

This explains the prominent role the video plays in this work. The narrator becomes obsessed with videotaping his body undergoing treatment, in the hands of doctors, and changing through disease. When the narrator imposes his video on the doctors, he reclaims his body for himself. He wants to film his doctor, Claudette Dumouchel, while she examines him. She refuses because she says she, too, will be in the picture and hates to be photographed. She claims his body for examination, but refuses hers to him on film. The triumph of the narrator comes when he makes the film and repossesses his body under examination by the Other.

In *The Compassion Protocol,* Guibert also enumerates many of his literary works. The narrator imagines that at his death, these miserable sheets of paper on which he writes will bring fortune. Visitors will come to his room, where they will find a plaque inscribed "It was here that Hervé Guibert wrote most of his books: *The Phantom Image, Singular Adventures, Arthur's Whims, Blindsight, You Made Me Create Phantoms, Incognito, The Compassion Protocol.*"[34] These lists serve as substitutes for the body as well. They also create a chronology of art, what will remain of Guibert once the body disappears. While disease ravages the body, artistic production reclaims the self. All that will remain after bodily decay is artistic creation. This very brief overview of some of Guibert's novels provides a chronological tour of his obsession with doubling.

Throughout his literary career, Guibert also wrote novels that incorporate photographs. This not only allowed him to showcase his two artistic talents, but also permitted him to complicate even further the doubling principles on which much of his literary work is based. In these texts, Guibert activates one of the primary realities of the medium, according to Barthes's model, in that he manipulates the inherent reality of photography. If photographs serve as "illustrations," they can elucidate the shifting narrative; but this is not the case with Guibert.

Written in 1979, *Vice* was not published until 1991, the year Guibert died. It juxtaposes photos and texts that do not seem to correspond one to the other. The introduction provides a definition of vice: "decor and acts," which places vice in the realm of the theatrical. The first section, "Articles personnels" (personal effects), provides brief written vignettes of everyday objects such as cotton balls, nail clippers, and tongue depressors. A "photo gallery," mainly of mannequins, follows this. The last written section, "un parcours" (a stroll), lists several vacant places in Paris such as Le Palais des Mirages (the Hall of Mirrors) and Le Musée de l'École de Médecine (the Medical School Museum). Guibert justifies an obsession with vacancy in this way: "From now on, the State should provide a certain number of vacant places with the sole intent of furthering small incursions into vice, into libertine ways, licentious specifically because of their time-wasting potential."[35] This text presents us, therefore, with a topology of pleasure.

The vices in this text are articulated on the principle of substitution: not the Freudian repression mechanism, but the erotic substitution inherent in fetishism. In the first section of the text, the ordinary objects listed become dangerous, or exciting, thus making them fetishistic substitutes for erotic pleasure with Sadean overtones. In Guibert's prose, cotton swabs not only clean ears, they also procure a "pleasant irritation" and can equally rupture the inner ear. The glove not only warms the hand, but also often serves to hide the prints of a strangler. Flypaper provides the ultimate "vice" because it attracts its victims to their death rather than repel them as citronella does. The most ordinary objects are viewed as objects of torture, but as alluring nonetheless.

The photo gallery that follows the section of personal items again underscores the bizarre nature of ordinary things. Guibert has photographed the ordinary storage areas of museums, and through juxtaposition and camera angles, he makes the objects they contain look bizarre. For instance, many of the photos contain heads, arms, and legs of dismembered mannequins. Nestled among these photos of limbs is a shot of sculpted busts waiting to be placed on pedestals. The busts recall the sculpture medium, but placed as they are, in rows waiting to be displayed, they have a disturbingly comic quality, of a world reversed, where the aesthetic becomes grotesque. An entire artistic medium becomes macabre through juxtaposition with the carnavalesque.

If we explore the photos in this text, many seem reminiscent of fetishism and its displacement of erotic impulse onto isolated parts of the object of desire. The fragmentation of the mannequins into body parts recalls Hans Bellmer's constructions, the surrealist artist most famous for his disturbing works with erotically positioned, often mutilated dolls. The eroticism of the fetishized objects becomes clear when Guibert features himself in the photo. Guibert is perhaps the voyeur aroused by the inanimate fragments.

The photos in this text are also substitutes for the text. The list of items described in the text before the photo gallery does not include the items listed in the photos. This would correspond to the theme of "vice" as Guibert has stated it. Vice represents vacant lack that the desired object must fill.

We can also link the fetishism of this text with a Sadean slant on sexuality.[36] Often in the text and in the photographs, the objects described subjugate the body. These ordinary objects of potential torture often have to do with medicine, such as the tongue depressor that chokes the patient, or the ether mask. Inanimate objects with harmful potential litter the seemingly empty spaces in hidden rooms.

The third and last segment of the text, "parcours," visits abandoned museums in Paris, mostly in a sort of all-encompassing view of the void, of vice. In his desire to tell all, a strategy Sade also embraced, Guibert provides a taxonomy of desire. In these sections, the *promeneur* alternates between Guibert's narrative "I" and an omniscient voyeur; the self and Other are both voyeurs of vice. The emptiness and lack of these places spurs desire that culminates in an orgasm of language. The verbal text of this section provides numerous lists of procedural details. For example, the taxidermist's workshop begins with a description of skins covering the workshop and hanging from the ceiling. Within this world filled with luxurious, tactile objects that are also frightening because of the deaths they represent, the taxidermist plods methodically through his procedures. He is absent from the workshop in this section of the text, however; only the work waits for his return.[37] Furthermore, many of the empty spaces chosen are filled with dismembered bodies and represent the storehouses of the fragmentation of desire. In another section of the text, the anatomy museum within the École de Médecine, the casual stroller that the narrator becomes encounters dismembered heads, skeletons, limbs resting on tables, wax figures, and bones of various human curiosities.[38] Among this group, Guibert notes models of vaginas, anuses, sexual parts of cadavers, and wax models. This last group explicitly introduces sexuality and sexual fetishism into this leisurely stroll through the halls of vice.

Scott Carpenter notes that for Sade:

[Vice] has little or nothing to do with that handful of pornographic expletives peppering Sade's prose. (Indeed, had Sade's texts been perceived as "mere" pornography, the authorities would have been more likely to peruse than to censor them.) Far more disquieting for the besieged classical sensibility was the preeminence of words meaning other than what they say, a trait common to both deceit and figurality. In Sade, such textual hypocrisy results in outrageous illusions: pure vice masquerades as virtue; or, as in *La philosophie dans le boudoir* (*Philosophy in the Bedroom*), philosophy dresses up as pornography. Masquerade is an essential component of libertinism, for the libertine always wears a veneer of virtue.[39]

For Guibert, vice is masquerade but also concealment of all kinds. Vice, inherent in the rooms filled with parts of bodies, unrecognizable objects, and mannequins, brings together the desire of the voyeur for wholeness and the role of the voyeur as actor. The photographer who strolls through these zones recording them reveals the pieces; desire allows the reader to fill the gaps, to make the object of desire whole. Projecting one's desire on the Other still leaves a void in partial need of satisfaction.

Published posthumously, *Lettres d'Egypte* (*Letters from Egypt*) compiles a series of letters Guibert wrote while on a trip to Egypt with the photographer Hans Georg Berger and includes a series of photos of Guibert, many of them self-portraits. Throughout this text, dating is denied (19__). Guibert remarks on the unreality of these dates, like those on a prison calendar (or, as we have seen in eighteenth-century novels where the texts masquerade as found objects).

This is a text of loss. Many of the letters refer to loss of sight. "I would be wise to describe things I have not seen, to fumble about like a blind person."[40] Others dwell on the impending death of Guibert's nonagenarian Aunt Suzanne. In many of the photographs, Guibert fractures himself in shots in which he inhabits the monuments of this lost culture, a spectacle of pleasure mediated through fragmentation.

Many of the letters in the text contain erotic information. He writes to lovers about whom he dreamed, and who remind him of objects he sees on his journey. This text suggests or reinforces the impossibility of inhabiting the Other, since distance from the object of desire creates a void. Longing to leave Egypt, but fearing a return to Paris, where the real letters he mailed his friends before embarking on his journey will go off "like bombs," he believes that taking photos of some of the sights he's witnessing in Egypt would be a violation because of the momentary nature of the act of snapping a photo. Longing, lack, and desire are mediated through letters and photos that make Guibert part of the eternal landscape. In the concluding image, Guibert photographs a hand, its prints visible on the windowpane above the digits, set against the landscape of Egypt's ancient ruins. The digital imprints leave the traces of the self and its simulacrum Other, a testimonial to desire, to lack, and to longing. They are Sade's secret cabinets and unimaginable manias of desire.

In several seminal essays, Lacan proposes models of the psyche that equate desire with life and the absence of desire with death. Guibert's impending death from AIDS made his desire more acute as he struggled to cling to life, a battle he waged with words and images. In *Camera Lucida,* Barthes writes, in front of a paragraph, our consciousness takes:

> The path of certainty: the Photograph's essence is to ratify what it represents . . . No writing can give me this certainty. It is the misfortune (but also perhaps the voluptuous pleasure) of language not to be able to authenticate itself . . . Every photograph is a certificate of presence.[41]

This may explain the ultimate conjunction of word and image in Guibert's work. Only the inclusion of photographs in his texts could assure him that his essence would continue to be present in the world.

Desire, intimacy, and public and private manifestations of sexuality all lead to possibilities for shifting body identity. Bringing sexuality to a public space, including the voyeur within the space of a usually private event, accelerates the possibility of multiple points of view. Within Sade and Guibert, sexuality plays itself out, characters assume roles and change roles within the textual space. Doublings of the self become visual as well, for Guibert especially, through photographs that not only take the place of texts but also assume the roles of the multiple selves. In *The Man in the Red Hat,* one of his last texts, paintings are substitutes, masks. Lovers have disappeared, but the narrator searches for visual works of art. The red hat he uses to hide his thinning hair and give himself a dashing aura is a prop that masks the loss of dignity. After the operation, the narrator remains swathed in bandages that dissimulate his body, whose identity has shifted toward disease. In this work, dissimulation is everywhere, the desire to pass for someone else. Masks become the reality of the narrator who defies his illness by assuming defiant identities. He loses his identity, but gains a theatrical persona: the anonymous man in the red hat. He passes, therefore, for a healthy person by hiding signs of illness. Like the forged paintings in the text, assuming an identity can devalue, but it can also protect.

Barthes notes photography's affinity to theater because both, for him, involve playing dead. He reminds us that the first actors separated themselves from the community by playing the role of the dead. Yet "however 'lifelike' we strive to make it (and this frenzy to be lifelike can only be our mythic denial of an apprehension of death), Photography is a kind of primitive theater, a kind of *tableau vivant*, a figuration of the motionless and made-up face beneath which we see the dead."[42] Sade brought a theatrical mind-set to his framework for understanding life. He staged bodies in sex acts, perhaps as a way to prove the author's ultimate control. Guibert uses the body itself as a stage, and the body assumes new identities. Roles shift in both authors: the voyeur becomes the actor, the narrator becomes the lover, desire makes bodies whole and gives them identity. In the end, fragments remain behind as remnants of shifting selves.

# 3

# Counting the Days: Hiding and Seeking to Pass the Time

Bodies exist in physical, spatial environments, and part of an understanding of individual identity is recognizing the body's spatial habitat. In the next chapter, we will study prisons and enclosures; when bodies are forced into limited spaces, they certainly modify their sense of identity. A sense of space goes hand in hand with sensitivity to the passage of time. Time's powerful force on bodies and their identities will be the focus of this chapter. The linear progression of time propels bodies forward, at least metaphorically, bringing the accumulated identity created and hopefully nurtured in the past toward a future, often unknowable.

Time's passage inevitably also modifies biological entities through growth to decline, decay, and death. Building up the body in youth, celebrating its strength, comes always with the knowledge that the moment will pass, that the body will weaken and perhaps fragment. The sense of identity built up through the body changes not only because of variations in social context, through masquerade, and acceptance or rejection of (sexual) Others and Otherness, but because time works on it. Time can also paradoxically be a weapon. The strong can use its passage to intimidate the weak; those living with decline can cling to it to slow it down.

Sade constructs a world in which time provides the framework for sex, for cruelty, and for power relationships. Time can be the victimizers' ally, allowing psychological tortures to have their desired effect. Idly passing time, a noble pursuit in pre-Revolutionary France, is represented when the four friends in the castle of Silling schedule the tortures according to a precise cycle. In *The 120 Days of Sodom*, time's passage is the primary torture, the inexorable inevitability of impending death for the victims. Bodies imprisoned in the castle know they have no escape, and the metaphorical ticking marks on the walls of their cells do not foretell a day of release, for only death is at the other end. Bodies are imprisoned by time.

Guibert's body is beholden to time for its survival. Trying to keep time from passing becomes a primary concern. For Guibert, time slips away as his body decays. He writes as a way to bring time to a halt, knowing the task is impossible. Time remains certainly the enemy as disease takes increasing hold of his body. Several of his texts include diaries, or false diaries, in an attempt to remember how his body became old, how disease took hold. It also allows Guibert to take note of the unnatural aging that so preoccupies him. A young man inhabits a body more suited to those of his great-aunts. Time is a personal enemy that Guibert hopes to tame by marking time explicitly in the text.

In some ways, this process represents the biography in reverse. We saw that in these two authors, biographies conceal as they reveal. Biographies supposedly also present a chronology of life events. But, whereas the biography challenges time by capturing the story of a human life, another aspect of both Sade and Guibert's work involves denying the story time to unfold.

Both authors' texts include a subtext of spending time and losing it. Telling stories, writing, recounting, and taking photos present ways of capturing the moment, of freezing time. In Sade's texts, however, telling stories not only makes time stop, it also can be lifesaving. The four storytellers in the castle of Silling, for example, have a privileged position with respect to other victims. They were chosen for their life experiences that could serve as examples of perversions to enlighten the company. They are as perverse in many ways as the four friends; their difference in social status within the castle is marked by their difference in social and economic status in the outside world. For Guibert, capturing the moment, writing or filming it—a theme more fully explored in the next chapter—becomes the only way to halt time's march.

This is also in some ways related to concealing and dissimulation. The body tries to shield itself from damage, from torture, disease, or decay, by denying the ontological reality of time's passage. With time, death is inevitable. Sade and Guibert explicitly try to halt time, to "manage" it, through narration.

## TIME SPENT AND LOST

Sade's victimizers use time as one more weapon they can wield against their victims. In a world where daily existence consists primarily of allowing one's body to be used at will in any fashion imaginable for the sexual gratification of others, time's passage is a blessing. Sade's torturers, rapists, mutilators, and murderers take complete control of bodies and try to erase their identities. As bodies succumb to progressively painful abuses, the victims become ever more merely victims, without specific identities. In some texts, characters retain their identities even after having lived through every imaginable evil; this is the case of the virtuous Justine. But she retains her identity precisely because she is an allegory of how virtue is doomed to failure. Just as in medieval allegory a virtue took the proper name of an object or person— the Rose, Everyman—Justine's name becomes a word to substitute with "victim." In the end, of course, she is annihilated, killed by lightning at the end of her travails. Even for her, the body cannot permanently assume the identity of victim and survive. Even more, Justine's comic ending, killed by one of the most arbitrary means possible after surviving unimaginable perils, is Sade's gesture of supreme disdain for the fundamental optimism of the philosophes.

For the torturers, time is a powerful tool, like the raping machine, to dehumanize the victim. By stretching out time, torturers prolong the pleasure that they need increasing stimulation to achieve. The knowledge of time's slow passage has the supplemental benefit of prolonging the suffering of the victim. In *The 120 Days of Sodom,* after the Duc of Blangis introduces the assembly to the organization of the tortures, emphasizing that their days will be organized hour by hour exclusively according to the will of the four friends, that they have no more family ties, no identities, are isolated and will, hourly, be abused reinforcing their servitude, the assembly bursts into tears.[1] Enslavement depends on the psychological torture of being at the mercy of a master timekeeper. In the end, the power relationships always mandated between characters in Sade's fiction lead to manipulation of time in the struggle to increase power.

In Sade's *120 Days of Sodom,* especially, counting days becomes akin to telling tales. We have already noted how the orgy

takes place over a very specific number of days, and how each
month has a unique focus, always gathering in intensity and cruelty. Also, each day is strictly divided according to a regime of
torture. With the precision of military geniuses, the friends devise
a schedule of activities beginning with a ten o'clock reveille, ending each night precisely at two o'clock in the morning. Each hour
of the day is dedicated to deflowering certain predetermined individuals, or sodomizing others, to eating meals, or to narrative
moments in the amphitheater.[2] This order serves also to heighten
the dreaded anticipation of victims as they await their inevitable
turn. Similarly, the weeks and months are arranged to heighten
the passage of time with festivals, forced marriages, and so forth.
This simulated gaiety provides a sarcastic structure to this society
"in reverse" in Silling.

Counting—obsessive numeration and numerological configurations—is one of the markers of Sade's *120 Days of Sodom.* One
study in particular provides an excellent overview of time and
counting in Sade; Peter Cryle, in *Geometry in the Boudoir. Configurations of French Erotic Narrative,* provides an elaborate
study of the numerology of *The 120 Days of Sodom,* its division of
time, and use of storytelling to mark time, which is a contrast to
the "out of time" fairy-tale tone. In his study comparing erotic
strategies in French eighteenth-century texts, he dedicates considerable energy to exploring Sade. With regard to the calculated
nature of Sade's erotic world, Cryle notes that Sade's texts are
particularly serious, "the very elaboration of an erotic discipline
depends on sustained and serious 'attention'."[3] Sade's practice
of numbers contributes to the serious tone of the text—Cryle relates this historically as well to the *ars erotica,* where numbers
mark the completeness of a set of figures.[4]

Cryle points to certain key numbers in Sade. The number one
thousand often signifies excess, "the number of unspeakable
events."[5] Four is a key number in organizing the events of the
text: four friends, four accomplished procuresses to recruit
women, four pimps to scout for men.[6] Crucially, four serves as a
key number not only at the beginning, when the administration
of the four-month ordeal is taking place, but also at the end,
when four executioners are torturing victims who find themselves in the middle of a performance of suffering organized by

the circle of four friends. Cryle continues to find this number in other texts such as *The Misfortunes of Virtue.*

The only number outside the foursome is six, the number of people recruited for the kitchen. Six women are dedicated to kitchen duties: three servants and three cooks. The former were executed at the end because "they earned it," but the three cooks were spared thanks to their talents. "The cooks and their aides will be respected, and the gentlemen who transgress this law will pay 1000 Louis fines."[7] At the end of the text, March 1, the friends decide to sacrifice the kitchen staff but save the three cooks.[8] As we have seen, they are among the residents of Silling not victimized or killed. Cryle points out that the six leftovers may allow for thirty victims to die, leaving sixteen residents spared: four squared.

Still, Cryle identifies miscalculations in the time frame for Sade's *120 Days of Sodom.* With Sade's relentless need to create a timetable for torture, complications arise not just:

> Because of the intractability of the calendar, but because Sade wishes to maintain rhythmic variations in intensity. There are weekly *fêtes,* where particularly festive punishments, mock marriages, and ritual deflowerings occur. The need to make extra time for the festivities means that each such day "is an event that results in the recounting of only four passions" (I, 373). Every time that a *fête* occurs, there must be narrative overtime on a working day, so that the extra passion can be recounted. Yet Sade often fails to make the proper compensating moves: he fails, so to speak, to measure the irregularity, so that we find him, at the end of the second, third and fourth sections of his manuscript asking himself in his notes to find out why there are too many or too few passions. In fact, to take but one example, there is one passion too many in the third quarter (I, 406). The net result, by my reckoning, of no fewer than five errors:
>   Days 2 and 9 of this section should have 4 passions, not 5 (they are *fêtes*).
>   Days 6 and 11 should have 5, not 4.
>   Day 15 should have 5, not 6.[9]

Certainly, the obsession with numbers indicates a need for order, control over the bodies of others being the primary mechanism of the torturers. For our purposes, it is the numerological precision of time that means the most. Sade clearly wants to use precise dating, ordering of temporal frameworks, to control time; here, not because the victims need more time, but because time will prolong their suffering. The events at Silling take place during the winter, in extreme darkness, in that location in the "Black Forest" far from France and hidden from view. Escape is impossible, given the roads made impassable by snow and the destruction of roads as the castle dwellers passed over them to prevent escape. The victims are selected to serve as victims and are alerted to their status before the party moves from France to Silling. So time cannot be on the victims' side. Calculating time, insisting on the length of time, serves as another torture. Specially prepared machines and methods honed in bordellos the world over provide new ways to victimize the wives and young people trapped in the castle. It is the slow passage of time itself, each segment marked off for all to see, that destroys their hope. Time's passage is one of the tortures, perhaps the most completed one, of Silling. Although there is an end, the relentless progression of events and days marks the impossibility of escape.

In Sade's fictional castle, the days and months mark the increasing intensity of torture. In Guibert's works, instead, time is the most precious commodity. Running out of time—for finding a cure, for writing—constitutes one of the important subtexts of much of his later work. Already in an early text, however, *Les Gangsters* (*Gangsters*), the way time ravages the body is projected onto the story of the family, in the biographical mode Guibert will continue to explore. He recounts the story of his two great-aunts, Suzanne and Louise, and gangsters who assail them. In a style reminiscent of the Nouveau Roman, they tell an incident, but the reader is led astray. The truth-value of the narrative is distorted through faulty memory and suspiciously untrustworthy narration. As was the case, for example, in Alain Robbe-Grillet's *Les Gommes* (*The Erasers*), clues are erased as the reader follows the narrator's path to an uncertain end. Temporal confusion exacerbates this journey.

Guibert frequently uses a partial diary format as a way to mark time in his texts. Although not complete, the precise references to some dates in the text allow the reader to enter into a rigorous time frame. Yet, the diary is often problematic in Guibert.

In his AIDS novels, the clearly delineated, rational use of the diary format creates order from chaos. Similarly, Guibert knows he risks losing his dignity, his sense of self, in the labyrinth of the hospital. He militantly refuses to capitulate. Order and strength are imposed on this world of illness. Guibert stakes out blocks of time for himself and clings to his body as it fades. In this way, time and self again intertwine.

Michael Denneny has noted that writers infected with HIV writing about AIDS have no parallel in previous literature:

> And while the closest parallel might be the poetry that came out of the trenches of the First World War, the bulk of that writing was published, reviewed and read after the war; whereas this AIDS writing is not only being produced in the trenches, as it were, but is being published, read by its public and evaluated by the critics in the midst of the crisis. It is as if Sassoon's poetry were being mimeographed in the trenches and distributed to be read by men under fire—the immediacy of these circumstances precludes the possibility of this being a merely aesthetic enterprise. The aesthetic requires distance and the distance is not available, not to the writer, not to the reader . . . in this onrush of death, posterity—even posterity as an imagined frame for the activity of writing—is a luxury.[10]

It is writing for the present, free of constraining cultural frameworks. Guibert's descriptions of his own dying body bear witness to this urgency. Yet Guibert's writing remains true to a very personal aesthetic, perhaps unlike other AIDS literature as noted by Denneny. Guibert's texts maintain the ebb and flow of a relationship with the aging body, as would happen with any writer whose primary focus is the body, but it is a bodily decay accelerated through disease. The body in Guibert's work assumes a transformative stance for a construction and deconstruction of self, from erotic encounters through disease. Guibert's writings create literary identity through AIDS. He manipulates time constructs to make them his. His writing contains within it the transformation of the AIDS pandemic. He filmed himself in the early 1990s in *La Pudeur ou l'impudeur* so that not only the words would "write until the end" but also the pictures, the camera eye, would preserve him forever.

The diary format represents perhaps the most intimate type of writing, in which the interior space of the author and the exterior space of the page fuse. We need only remember the personal diaries of Frida Kahlo, Anne Frank, or Virginia Woolf to understand the power of this form. Yet the diary has always presented certain ambiguities when it becomes literature, when it is marketed to be consumed by an audience larger than one. The *journal intime* as literature is often a wry commentary on the nature of the public consumption of literature, as much as it is about the ideas of the author.

Guibert is an author, one could say, whose entire production has as its very theme the nature and shifting paradigms of intimacy itself. His works are always a dissection of intimacy. An early text, *Voyage avec deux enfants,* presents itself as a diary, a travelogue of adventures. Using a narrative strategy akin to the asterisks after Sade's Bishop's name, the narrator begins by telling us "the origin of the voyage goes back to Sunday, March 14, 19. . . ."[11] The first entry begins Friday, March 19, with no year. Already the time of narration and the time of exposition do not coincide. The last entry is from Saturday, April 10, but a "Part III" follows where the narrator breaks away from the voyage. The text ends with an anecdote of a man on the Metro writing a letter; he had gone away "just to be able to write, to be able to write to me that he had left."[12] By writing, he understands his day has not been useless. It is by writing down his departure that the voyage becomes complete. After a text recounting a fantastic voyage, the banal metro excursion becomes the pretext for a text because that journey too means leaving, but leaving also behind a written trace of oneself. Writing reveals itself the true impetus of the disturbing, phantasmagoric voyage with two children who become objects of sexual fantasies. Being able to say all is the pretext.

The diary format anchors the voyage into a temporality just as the voyage moves forward in space. Still, while largely moving forward day by day, the chronology of this text backtracks. From the first March 19, for example, we return to March 13 to find the roots of the voyage. Although in general chronologically linear, this first Guibertian diary text presents time as a problematic phenomenon.

Guibert's use of the diary format in several of his works in which he discusses AIDS reveals much about the way in which the author has reworked the diary format and inverted it to some extent. Intimacy becomes risky after AIDS, and allowing the chronological progression of the diary to unravel thwarts the risks incurred in the diary format. In *Fou de Vincent* (1988), written when Guibert had just been diagnosed HIV-positive, Guibert recounts the progressive discovery that his most recent lover has AIDS. The text is written in what seems to be a diary format, with explicit dates, but in fact the dates contradict themselves. Information is subverted in the text, inverted, so that intimacy can be preserved for the purely personal space. The subject of AIDS, and the fear of intimacy it suggests, mirror the fear of revealing oneself in a truly intimate literary genre, the diary.

In his penultimate work, *Cytomegalovirus: A Hospitalization Diary* (1992), Guibert chronicles his last stay in the hospital as he confronts the virus of the title that causes blindness, among other complications. This diary is excessive because Guibert races against time. In fact, the diary here serves as a witness to the impossibility of intimacy. Erotic feeling returns, only to be suppressed when the sexual act becomes impossible because of weakness and medication. The body's identity as sexual being disintegrates, and with it a measure of hope. All that remains is decaying flesh. The diary becomes an ironic commentary on the nature of intimacy.

For Ross Chambers, "AIDS journals, in their turn—although they do not have the status of legal evidence, as Holocaust witness sometimes does—are similarly a form of testimonial writing whose subject is dead. In them a mortally afflicted individual (in almost every instance known to me a gay man) gives a firsthand report of the process of his own demise."[13] He notes that,

As a witnessing discourse, AIDS diaries challenge some conventional understandings of both the diary form and the genre of autobiography. As diary explicitly and openly conceived with a view to publication—having publication as its essential finality—does not exclude the practice of intimate self-analysis associated with the *journal intime,* but it radically changes its orientation and significance by questioning the public-private dichotomy by virtue of which the "personal" diary is defined. And an autobiography that gives priority to a witnessing impulse over the memorializing function—the retrospective construction of a "life" in its narrative configurations that might be thought characteristic of classical autobiographies—seems a departure from the genre's defining origins, while, finally, the immediacy of reporting and the episodicity of form that AIDS diaries (like other diaries) espouse simultaneously distinguish them formally from the narratives of witness.[14]

A note on word usage: in English, we distinguish the words *journal* and *diary*. Although dictionaries describe both as "a daily record written of one's experiences," the diary also includes "feelings." English usage distinguishes *journal* also as a substitute for *newspaper*, although this usage is rare. In French, the word *journal* is at once always the newspaper, that is, the public record of factual events, and a personal space for recording "the daily recounting of events." The *journal intime*, as described by Sarah Lowe in the introduction to Frida Kahlo's recently published diary, is a "private record written by a woman for herself."[15] The overlap between public and private telling, public and private spaces in which intimacy can flourish, is evident in the choice of terms. With regard to Guibert's two texts under consideration here, *Fou de Vincent* is once explicitly described as a "journal," and *Cytomegalovirus* is subtitled *Journal d'Hospitalisation*. The choice of the word *journal* is essential because Guibert plays on the public/private duality.

Irrespective of the term we use, what we call a diary in published form always has certain characteristics. As Christina Baldwin has noted, the journal always presents dated entries so the writer can record the passage of time. The diary builds a point of observation of us. We are both subject and object of the gaze. This, however, according to Baldwin, does not predicate self-division, but glorification of the multiplicity of the self. She states that the "journal's capacity to track down what is happening with our lives increases our sensitivity to our needs"[16] and that would allow the journal to have a therapeutic effect. The connections between journal entries are often mysterious, mimicking the flow of writing. As we shall see, this mystery is increased in Guibert since he subverts the expectations of the diary format.

Ultimately, the journal is about time, marking time and its passage—or its negation. In *Fou de Vincent*, Guibert relates his relationship with Vincent, about whom he is crazy, as the title indicates. This is the first of Guibert's texts in which AIDS plays an explicit role. In previous works, various characters were depicted as having mysterious illnesses, but in this text, Vincent's lesions are diagnosed as AIDS-related.[17] The narrator/Guibert is paranoid about contracting the disease from his lover. Only toward the end of the text does he reveal that he fears he is infected. This subtext of disease is interspersed with explicit sexual encounters between the two and the joyous feelings that they arouse.

The novel presents the amorous encounters of Vincent, a bisexual drug addict, and the narrator; the presence of AIDS rhythms this erotic work. The narrator, the foil for Guibert, is both curious and afraid of the way in which the disease begins to affect the body of his lover. In several scenes the narrator examines, often surreptitiously, the lesions that appear on his lover's body. In an early part of the text, while they make love, the narrator expresses his desire for a condom; Vincent protests "you're really scared of getting AIDS, aren't you?"[18] At this juncture, AIDS looms over them but has not touched them; it exists only as a nightmare. The narrator then has a sexually explicit dream in which "I dream: Vincent sucks me, at last, I am able to put my prick in his mouth. I notice that under his tongue he has little white stars that must have escaped from the starry globe I left on so I could fall asleep."[19] The narrator's fantasy of experiencing the "active" sexual role for the first time in the relationship becomes a nightmare of unknown disease symptoms. Illness still presents itself as a pleasurable experience, however, as stars that escaped from the starry globe of a lightbulb, the last refuge from the ominous, dark night for the narrator who left it on. This protective light becomes the menacing white lesion on the infected lover. In this passage, disease invades nightmares and the preconscious level of the psyche.

Soon, however, it becomes clear that Vincent is sick. At the beginning of the section of the text from 1988, the narrator recounts Vincent telling him, "I have fungus, he said; I have scabies, he said; I have the clap, he said; I have lice; and I pulled his body to mine."[20] Vincent's stories appear unreliable, just as false narration characterizes the whole text. He recites symptoms that have no clinical validity. He tries to hide his disease through an almost *reductio ad absurdum*; it seems as though Vincent is stricken with everything. Perhaps for that reason, the narrator still succumbs to his charms and pulls him close. The diseased body remains fascinating for both characters.

Later in the text, Vincent reveals that he is taking antibiotics to

cure blotches on his feet. After Vincent goes to the local dermatologist, the narrator tells us, "It's a fungus that he waited too
long to medicate, I shouldn't touch it, it's not really very conta-
gious, but we should be careful."[21] Despite the caution imposed
by Vincent's visit to the doctor, who represents an official voice
against disease, the narrator takes a voyeuristic pleasure in
seeing these lesions. This is the point where Vincent begins to
think he has AIDS. This is also when the narrator begins to doubt
Vincent's stories. As the nature of the disease becomes clear, the
narrator's stance toward Vincent also changes. Although the narrator takes pleasure in the lesions, after they make love, he
changes all the sheets and sprinkles antifungal powder on them.
He himself goes to the dermatologist, to whom he lies, stating
that he may have been infected by a one-night stand. The doctor
affirms that no fungus in the world would have taken the form
described to him as seen on Vincent. Finally, Vincent reveals to
the narrator that he has AIDS.[22]

All telling and retelling is suspect in this novel. Even medical
discourse can prove unreliable. Vincent's initial report from the
doctor diagnoses the fungi, but the doctor whom the narrator
consults denies the possibility of that hypothesis. The only "witness" is the spots and the deformities the disease produces on
the body. In effect, the progression of the disease is the only part
of the text whose chronological order is not reversed. In revealing
Vincent's disease, the narrative moves from first manifestation of
the disease to avowal of AIDS.

*Fou de Vincent* presents itself as a journal, one in which the
narrator works through his relationship to Vincent. Several references to dates, years only, are presented in the margins of the
text, set off from the preceding text by a white space. These years
begin with 1988 and move backward chronologically to 1982 (the
year the narrator tells us he first met Vincent). The first years—
1988, 1987, 1986, that is, the most recent time frame—represent
the longest passages of this scant text. The following dates—1985,
1984, 1983, and 1982—are all mentioned within the last eight
pages of the text, thus accelerating time as it falls backward. No
months or days are mentioned in these marginal inscriptions.
The text does, however, begin by mentioning specific days: "During the night between November 25 to 26, Vincent fell from a
fourth story window while playing parachute with his bath-

robe."[23] The imperfect tense in the text, as evidenced in the quotation above, is another marker of time's fluidity, even its
circularity. To relate events that happened at a precise time in the
past, French prefers the passé composé tense (or passé simple in
historical texts). The imperfect narrates events begun in the past,
continuing, habitual, or repeated events in the past, or an event
spanning over time while another, finite event in the past took
place. Guibert's use of the imperfect tense, "Vincent tombait," in
a context with a precise date, "du 25 au 26 novembre," is un-
usual, even ungrammatical. He puts the accent on the duration
of the event, on its extension into the present. It is not an action
completed in the past, ended with the death of Vincent, but an
action that continues, perhaps, to influence the narrator. That
may be why the narrator begins by recalling Vincent's fall, not
his death. The latter is irreversible. Time did not stop, was not
demarcated clearly, simply because the narrator used a precise
date. The diary's precision is already contradicted through verb
usage.

The first paragraph of the text also mentions November 27.
These very explicit dates set out the parameters for Vincent's
death due to the fall described above, which was induced by a
drug overdose. The second paragraph mentions that the narrator
met Vincent in 1982, and Vincent became an obsession for six
years. These dates set out the parameters of the relationship.
Specific references to months and days, but not to years, create
an objective temporality. They are the only signposts that give
this text an exterior "legitimacy." We could check the dates of
Vincent's death objectively in a biography.

The only other references to time in the text are deictic: such
expressions as "hier soir" (yesterday evening), "pour deux ou
trois jours" (for two or three days), etc. These references have
meaning only with regard to the interior workings of the text.
They are signposts of the intimacy of the text.

Between these two poles lie the years written in the margins of
the text. Historical time and diary time coincide as these pages
chronicle the years Vincent and the narrator spent together.
Within this space, however, the descriptions of AIDS form the
scaffolding. In the section of the text prior to the one marked
1988, the narrator notes that Vincent no longer has the red marks
on his back he had a month previously. He later notes that Vin-

cent has small white blotches under his tongue. In the section from 1988, Vincent continues to try to hide the lesions that appear on his body or to make light of them. Yet in the section from 1987, Vincent admits he has AIDS. The chronological presentation of illness is muddled. When the reader first reads about allusions to disease, its nature is unclear. We then discover, however, that the previous year, Vincent had already revealed he has AIDS. Our linear progression through the text clashes with the chronology of disease. The reader's expectations are thus thwarted by the diary format.

The narrator alternates between loving acceptance of the news of Vincent's infection and paranoid behavior, such as cleaning the sheets he and Vincent slept in with antiseptic powder once Vincent leaves. It seems in the early part of the text that the narrator is terrified of Vincent's infecting him. Yet in the section from 1985, the narrator admits that he is sure he's infected. This would suggest that in fact he had infected Vincent. We see that in this text, references to time suggest a history of disease that is then proven erroneous.

The events chronicled in the text do not move from most distant to most recent. The narrator tells us toward the end of the text, "I'm running so late in this notebook that I now have to tell two evenings with Vincent, each of which is a bit the opposite of the other."[24] He admits to a conscious structuring effort in this text, to an explicit ordering mechanism. It is as though these two stories, the erotic one and the diseased one, were "à l'envers," mirror images of one another. In the same way, the text is a mirror, where details from the beginning of the relationship are projected onto the end of the book and vice versa. The narrator unself-consciously tells us he is ordering his stories as he tells them. After Vincent's death, he decided "to find him in these notes, backwards."[25] The narrator's ruse leaves the reader doubting the validity of any of the information in the text. What seems autobiographical, a discovery of the self's erotic body, may be "only fiction."

In this text, the narrator and Vincent negotiate their roles constantly. The narrator blurs the existential parameters between them as their love affair evolves. In an analogous fashion, chronology of infection—which of the two protagonists is sick first—becomes confused in the mind of the reader. These ontological erasures take place on a literary level largely due to the manipulations of temporal markers in the playful diary format. Guibert confounds our expectations of clarity so that we must enter his world.

The subtext of *Fou de Vincent* is the centrality of the act of writing, a theme explored further in the next chapter. Guibert notes that he is writing a travel notebook of his love for Vincent. Time and space travel merge in the diary. He also suggests he is creating a text for his lover on the model of Roland Barthes's *A Lover's Discourse*. Barthes posits a special language for lovers, composed of figures, fragments of linear discourse put together to express various nuances of the emotion of love. These figures are like gestures or acts, impulsive and incomplete. It is a way of speaking through the body.[26] *Fou de Vincent* is a text fragmented through time and a love story told through the body. Guibert's text is a study in the erotic pleasure of the text and the body, both erotic landscapes for a travelogue.

In *Fou de Vincent*, Guibert attempted to make time go backward from death to the moment of love, from 1988 to 1982. The years accelerate as they move backward in time, as though the details were more difficult to grasp. Time, an obsession for Guibert in these AIDS novels, may be moving backward as well. In *Fou de Vincent*, Guibert may be attempting to arrest his own death through recapturing the time of love.

*Cytomegalovirus: A Hospitalization Diary* also presents itself as a diary. Written from a hospital bed as Guibert was fighting the virus that threatened to blind him, the text is divided into segments, with month and day used occasionally as headings. There are, however, no indications of years in this text. The reader must deduce that the year was 1991, given Guibert's death date. He spent twenty-two days in the hospital, from September 17 to October 8, when he was released for home health care. As was the case for *Fou de Vincent*, each entry in this text is not of the same length, but those at the beginning of his stay (the first three days) and those at the end (the last eight days) are the most abbreviated. The days in between represent the most crucial for Guibert, those in which he begins to take control of his hospital environment, and during which he undergoes an operation to save his sight.

In *Cytomegalovirus: A Hospitalization Diary*, similar in structure to *Fou de Vincent,* the diary becomes excess; the author fastidiously marks the passage of events and of time through the use of the diary format. In fact, the diary here serves as a witness to the impossibility of intimacy; only at the end of the text do erotic feelings return to the author, which are dashed when he discovers the medication he had been taking will make him impotent. Intimacy, perhaps even sexual identity, no longer exists in this world in which the patient is under the microscope, and the diary becomes an ironic commentary on the nature of intimacy.

The crucial issue during the stay is whether or not the cytomegalovirus that has invaded his body will render him permanently blind. Blindness means not being able to read and not being able to write. Writing, like the IV pole Guibert desperately clings to, becomes a lifeline. As Guibert tries to navigate the hospital, he comes to see the IV pole as a weight, but he also knows it provides him life-giving fluid. He wants to write, but he only has access to a pencil nub. He jealously hides it from nurses who try to discard it as they straighten the room. Preserving dignity is one of the central themes of the text, being allowed to live on one's own terms. As was the case in an earlier AIDS text, *The Man in the Red Hat,* where the red hat symbolizes an attempt to hide receding hair and maintain a handsome outward appearance, in *Cytomegalovirus: A Hospitalization Diary,* Guibert is incensed that he receives only one spoon with which to eat both soup and yogurt. The ultimate affront of the hospital is the necessity of wearing the flimsy hospital gown. Guibert rails against the seemingly small indignities that erode his sense of self.

The need to reclaim his hospital space is constantly emphasized as another way of maintaining dignity. Guibert spends much time and detail recounting how he fought to be given an IV pole that moved so that he could walk with his pole instead of being immobilized in his bed. He also is quite concerned with obtaining a writing table, and both of these immediate needs spark descriptions of the various personnel in the hospital. Certain nurses and orderlies are singled out for ridicule given their treatment of the patient, others for praise. In the end, he obtains both the tools he needs.

These objects become crucial to tying the discussion of the hospital to the larger issue of writing. Guibert is obsessed with recording everything that happens to him, which will allow him to retain his dignity in the face of the humiliating circumstances in the hospital. Guibert must have the writing table, must be free to move and explore within the hospital. The writing table, his pencil and pad, the IV pole, and the various tubes used to feed and hydrate him all become lifelines for his body and toward writing. Much of the description in the pages dedicated to days related at greatest length involves obtaining and fighting for these objects. They come to represent the body, since it has no more physical reality for him. In fact, what is at stake for him is writing, since he may go blind, and the end of writing, Guibert suggests on the last page, is the end of life for him. Reclaiming the body will only be part of the battle. The real issue is reclaiming the self from the dehumanized world of the hospital.

Each passing day becomes the object of reflection, but are these reflections really a "journal"?[27] Yes, in that they encapsulate the ambiguity of the French word: a private writing space and a public factual space. Guibert records the events, the minute personal details of his life in the hospital, but not as an end unto themselves. This is not a journal intime, destined only for private consumption. It represents a public stand against the dehumanization of the hospital, a stand against dying quietly, against going gentle into that good night, as poet Dylan Thomas eloquently wrote. Guibert records the facts of hospital life to make them public, as an outcry against mistreatment. Also, it is against the decay of his body that he rails. By writing, he recaptures the body. In a gesture that links Sade and Guibert, he tells us that "writing is also a way of giving rhythm to time and a way to pass it."[28] At the end of his stay, as blindness encroaches, he is so frustrated by difficulty reading that he forces himself, he devours texts.[29] The insatiable appetite for saying, for the creative act, is one with the survival instinct. Cytomegalovirus: A Hospitalization Diary is a journal or diary, a journal or newspaper as in French, a subjective and an objective account of a harrowing time, recorded for all time.

For Stéphane Grisi, "the autopathographic writer exposes himself to the reader to find confirmation of his existence after the declaration of illness."[30] Guibert's journal may very well conform to this definition of "autopathography" in that it takes a militant stand toward the dehumanization of the body as it dies, the cruel dissolution of the sense of identity inherent in the body.[31]

*Fou de Vincent* and *Cytomegalovirus: A Hospitalization Diary* are linguistically similar. They mimic the language of an unpublished diary by interspersing long, almost ungrammatical sentences with short prepositional phrases and sentence fragments. They represent the discourse of the mind. In *Fou de Vincent,* this technique may mimic the fragmented lover's discourse; in *Cytomegalovirus: A Hospitalization Diary,* it may imitate the breathing body clinging to life. In both, the style creates the feel of a private writing that will know a public readership. In that way, the diary has an element of theatricality, of bringing the potentially private on stage. In both texts, Guibert uses the diary format to thwart our expectations of the diary. He manipulates the form, the temporal elements of it, to elongate time. Maybe by manipulating time in this way, he controls it, creating more of it for himself.[32]

In 2001, Guibert's actual diary was published as *Le Mausolée des amants. Journal 1976–1991.* In a preface note, Christine Guibert, Hervé's wife, wrote that Hervé himself typed the manuscript up to page 503 and that she completed it before submitting it to Éditions Gallimard.[33] This gesture itself shows that Guibert's intent was in fact to reveal all. Whether Guibert's transcription represents the actual content of his diary remains irrelevant: most probably, as had always been the case with his work, this text may rearrange factual evidence to highlight aspects important to Guibert. In any case, the authenticity of the text is less important than the authorial will to publish these most private moments. Many diaries are published posthumously without the author's consent; this is clearly not the case here. Just as Guibert orders time to construct a narrative in many of his obviously fictional works, here he takes control of his last text with his waning forces, the text of his life as lived. Still, the reader cannot help but wonder at the extent of fictionalization in these pages. Is this not, in fact, the testimonial, the tombstone, the mausoleum for lovers? The central project of life, if we consider the title, has always been to tell the tale of the body in love, until its dying breath.

Guibert's film *La Pudeur ou l'impudeur,* produced before his death, provides another view of the relentless need to "say everything" about the body. He records his body performing the banal acts of shaving or doing exercises, as well as attempting suicide. The film, aired on French television a month after he died, captured the physicality of Guibert's body in decay, freezing it for all time. The image as seen by the video camera not only captures fleeting moments forever, it also allows the author/director to leave a trace of himself. Guibert's use of the video camera to record his body dying of AIDS left a potent mark on the French viewing public, as noted by the controversy of the first showing of the video on national television a month after Guibert died.

In *The Compassion Protocol,* the video camera also plays an important role. As he navigates the hospital, trying to find a cure, and continues to travel to experience life as he already feels his body weakening, recording life on video becomes essential. The narrator becomes obsessed with videotaping his body undergoing treatment in the hands of doctors and changing through disease. Especially intense are moments when Guibert wants to videotape his doctor, Dumouchel, whom he finds attractive and powerful. With respect to the doctor-patient relationship, Caron has noted that videotaping plays a double role in the text. On the one hand, it allows Guibert to affect the reader's point of view by reproducing in the text the narcissistic gaze of the narrator; "on the other hand, it deeply modifies the relation between doctor and patient by inserting the possibility of a second, competing gaze, that of the patient, onto the doctor. The appearance of the camcorder in the doctor's office disrupts a relationship previously based on the nonreciprocity of the medical gaze."[34]

Videotaping the body becomes the way to own it again. When the narrator imposes his video on the doctors, he reclaims his body for himself. He wants to film his doctor, Dumouchel, while she examines him. She refuses because she says she, too, will be in the picture and hates to be photographed. She claims his body for examination but refuses hers to him on film. The triumph of the narrator comes when he makes the film and repossesses his body under examination by the Other. The narrator states that:

> I changed the angle of the take, and, without even asking her permission, I filmed Claudette Dumouchel. She was beautiful. I filmed her long white hands that were tapping the keyboard of her computer. I filmed her face in that sublime radiance, I was so happy. With my eye to the eyepiece, I saw that the image was trembling slightly to the rhythm of my breathing, the beatings of my heart. The word "End" began to flash in the viewfinder. End of cassette.[35]

This triumphant reclamation is the last scene of the novel. The symbolic, blinking word *end* represents the closure of video, text, and soon, life.

The videotape brings the body into view, but it also stages the body (as did the journal to some extent). In fact, Ross Chambers understands the video image as part of rhetoric of performance, in a sense, as a way of understanding the self. Chambers'

> [R]eading of *La pudeur ou l'impudeur* will therefore necessarily be a reading of the video's rhetoric, of the plastic wrapping that makes it—with its "decent" structures of address and its representational fakery—an exemplary *representation*, "au plus près de la mort," of the dying of an author and so, for the reader (viewer), a site of confrontation with death.[36]

He continues, "I emphasize the video's rhetoricity, then, only because I wish to establish its status as an act of witness, an act inevitably bound up with the politics, the poetics, and the aesthetics of representation, because representation is a means of survival, and so of prolonged efficacy for the witnessing act."[37] As was the case with the journals, this last video remains an act of defiance, daring the viewers to appropriate the body as it decays. This polemic stance may be the best way for the body to reaffirm its identity, by reflecting it back at the passive viewer as an object for scrutiny. As was the case with Guibert's—and Kahlo's— aggressive self-portraits, these later "truthful" works present a last attempt at living to the end.

Denneny states that virtually all the writers he knows of "who have grappled with AIDS in their work . . . use the imagination and the capacities of language and its forms to comprehend what is happening."[38] Although Guibert's writings after he was diagnosed as HIV-positive fit this general description of AIDS literature, they remain very similar in theme and scope to his previous works. His career-long obsession with the body remains, it merely refocuses on the dying body. Guibert becomes militant against those in the medical establishment who would appropriate his body. He refuses to allow them to possess him as an object of study. He maintains his right to an eroticized body. Writing and the eroticized body remain links to life in Guibert's works.

The body's shifting identity remains ultimately an issue of power, as Butler would have it. Mastering time remains of the essence: for Sade, dominators use time to subjugate victims; in Guibert, the dying man manipulates time to remain alive. Guibert fights the hospital and the doctors for the power to control as much of his body as he can so he can be granted a bit more time. Sade and Guibert are both clever in how they manipulate time: Guibert in order to extend life (so therefore in some ways his suffering), and Sade to extend the suffering of his victims. But this entails radically different subject positions. Although Sade often uses his role as imprisoned libertine to try to elicit sympathy for his status as victim, in his writings, the libertine controls time through imprisoning the captives' bodies. The Sadean text approaches time from the position of all-powerful subject. Guibert instead especially in later texts, falls victim to time despite desperate attempts to control it through the use of the diary form and the videocamera. In the end, time runs out, as the word *end* flashes before the eye.

# 4

# Imprisoned Bodies / Liberating Narratives

Bodies, restrained and progressively limited in their movement, have been an underlying element of the preceding chapters. For the body to lose its sense of identity, to be limited to acting on a stage—actual or metaphorical—and to have its sense of time counted to keep it functioning all in the end pose limits to mobility. In fact, the body in Sade and Guibert can be understood as imprisoned. For Sade, confinement is part of the torturer-victim dialectic. Although Guibert's early texts start closer to Sade's perspective, in his AIDS texts, the aging ill body itself becomes a prison.

In Sade's life, imprisonment and writing were linked. He wrote the majority of his works during his long periods of incarceration. Some critics say that Sade's need to write stems from rage at the body's chains. To some critics, the anger in Sade's texts is largely humorless, an expression of the anger at humankind's captivity.[1] Within Sade's works, too, prisons, convents, monastic cells, and dungeons abound as places that house and provide a space for erotic fantasies. Sexuality and imprisonment are linked. Enclosing the body provides the material of the text that will in turn be born in enclosure.

Guibert's body dying of AIDS, the sexuality that keeps it alive, and the act of writing are all also linked. Perhaps the most poignant example is *Cytomegalovirus: A Hospitalization Diary*. As his body lies trapped in a hospital during a stint to try to cure him of the virus that may make him blind, Guibert continues to lust for beautiful bodies—of nurses, of fellow patients, and so forth. Weary, however, in the end, he concludes that sexuality is impossible. Sexuality, the theme of his works, and writing are both acts of survival for Guibert, especially as he enters the end of his life.

Although Sade's body is imprisoned, Guibert is imprisoned within his own diseased body; for both, writing provides freedom.

Furthermore, in both authors' works, the act of storytelling bestows life. In *The 120 Days of Sodom,* four storytellers are among the cast of victims chosen by the four friends who mastermind the four-month orgy at Silling, of which the text is a day-by-day retelling. Like Scheherazade in the *Arabian Nights,* the Florentine *brigata\** in Boccaccio's *Decameron,* or the pilgrims in the *Canterbury Tales,* these tellers' function is to entertain the guests every evening with words. The legendary sexual exploits of these four old women made them ideal as soothsayers for the libertines' entertainment. With these retellings of their own sexual lives, they provide virtually the only form of spontaneous nonphysical contact in this spectacle of preordained rituals of sexual enslavement. Their words are the only moments of freedom for the victims. The old lady storytellers of this text may have their precursor in Sorel's *Histoire comique de Francion* in which the aged and hideous Agathe—former prostitute, current madam, and indefatigable storyteller—relates the adventures of her protégée Laurette, mistress of deception. Sade seems therefore to be writing in a familiar context, one with which he enjoys playing. Libertine comic novelists before Sade were also interested in playing with forms, and he may be consciously misusing form to push the Enlightenment over the brink. He shares a similar rejection of received ideas and conventions with the libertine writers who went before him.

In Guibert, writing substitutes for the body as it withers. Writing until the end makes life and writing coincide. The last years of his life produce a furious flurry of texts. In one of the last entries in Guibert's collected diary pages from *Le Mausolée des amants,* his last work to be published, Guibert seems to make a pact with himself: "Three books under construction is a bit too much. But as long as they are under construction, they are a pretext for not killing myself."[2] Guibert's only reason for living, for not ending it, is writing until the end.

---

*In the *Decameron,* a wealthy group of Florentines, known collectively as "la brigata" or "brigade," escape the plague by leaving the city. To pass the time, they each relate stories.

## Torture Chambers

Prisons, enclosures that confine rather than protect, permeate
Sade's landscape. In these texts, characters are trapped against
their will to ensure they will become victims. Fortresses in the
woods, dungeons, and convents where inhabitants do more than
pray abound. It is difficult, therefore, to speak of Sade without
mentioning this omnipresent theme. Characters find themselves
literally enclosed in spaces that menace them, so space, like time
as we have seen in the previous chapter, is necessary for the dialectic of victim to victimizers. Bodies are controlled, both in time
and in space. Limited, they begin to lose their materiality. Lever
notes certain themes that Sade would go on to develop until they
became the hallmark of his style: "the pleasure principle, confinement, and what he would come to call 'isolism,' his word for
the radical impossibility of communication between human beings."[3] In both the libertine's life and works, enclosed spaces of
all kinds restrain the body in its quest for unlimited sexual freedom. In life, writing became Sade's escape; his literary career
began during his years of incarceration. In his literary works,
prisons usually restrain victims as they are forced to live through
the sexual fantasies of others, much more so than providing enclosures for punishing victimizers' transgressions.

De Beauvoir understands Sade's incarceration as the beginning of a career as writer. She also alludes to his obsessive numeration, as explored in the previous chapter. Perhaps this
compulsive behavior springs from the need to count his own
captivity. The slow passage of time adds to the victim's torture,
but it also tortures Sade as he creates phantoms in his cell. De
Beauvoir also notes that imprisonment would have been particularly difficult for Sade precisely because sexuality is public.
"Sade's sexuality is not a biological matter. It is a social fact. The
orgies in which he indulged were almost always collective affairs.
In Marseilles he asked for two prostitutes and he was accompa-
nied by his valet."[4] In this way, we could explain Sade's plea to
his wife that he must give life to sexual phantoms. The prison
does not allow his fantasies to be realized; only shadows of fantasies remain.

What of this writing that takes place in the prison? What does
Sade's writing say about his prison, his writing born as it was in

incarceration and continuing through his life, spanning several different political regimes? Sade, after all, lived adventures before he became a writer, but the impulse to bring what he had lived to paper comes only when it is most difficult to write. He lacks materials in prison, although he doesn't lack time. For de Beauvoir, "Literature enabled Sade to unleash and fix his dreams and also to transcend the contradictions implied by any demonic system. Better still, though, it is itself a demonic act, since it exhibits criminal visions in an aggressive way. That is what gives it its incomparable price."[5] Sade's writing may indeed be an act of aggression, a demonic act. He brings to life his fantasies precisely when the prison impedes him from living them. In that way, Sade's writing becomes like his use of time as seen in the previous chapter. Sade must control and make his words permanent, just as he used time to enslave his victims. Writing allows control of imagined acts that cannot be put into action. That could be the motivation behind the obsessiveness of Sade's writing—the excessively long narratives, the use of any and all means to write even without proper materials—while in prison. Writing is a release, the only release, in a very sexual way. Writing provides the orgasm Sade kept searching for, the ultimate thrill. As Barthes has mentioned, writing can be "jouissance." In Sade's texts, the characters are constantly trying to "décharger," to come, and the urge to do so propels the victimizers to search endlessly and everywhere for victims. This is only a temporary release, however, which explains the compulsion for characters to come repeatedly, and of Sade to write incessantly. Writing is the release, the *décharge*, when sexual release is impossible.

Perhaps for Sade, writing is about rendering concrete— "réaliser" in French—as he suggested he needed to do in the letter to his wife. To render something concrete in English implies a kind of architecture, a building process. Like an idea, a structure becomes solid when it is rendered concrete. "Réaliser" (a false cognate for the English "to realize") instead implies taking something immaterial and transforming it into a tangible reality. The ephemeral nature of Sade's sexual obsession, of his dreams that must be realized, gains its physical reality in the written page. Writing in prison, therefore, is the only way for Sade to continue his identity as master of bodies.

Giving bodies to his phantoms, bringing back an element of

materiality to all that is by force of bodily restraint only a phantom, can be achieved through writing. This is a supremely egotistical move, trying to "have it all" and "say it all." Perhaps, however, that is a necessary characteristic of the project of writing one's fantasies. For Albert Camus, "The writer, of course, has no need to refuse himself anything. For him, at least, boundaries disappear and desire can be allowed free rein. In this respect Sade is the perfect man of letters. He created a fable in order to give himself the illusion of existing."[6] Writing from the prison becomes the moment of real freedom for Sade.

Writing to excess is madness, but it is also the only liberation. Blanchot contextualizes this freedom inherent in saying everything by remembering the political climate that forced Sade into prison, from where he would "say everything. This line alone would have been sufficient to render him suspect, this project to condemn him, his realization to imprison him. And Bonaparte should not be held responsible. We always live under a First Consul, and always Sade is persecuted and always because of the same exigency: saying everything, you have to say everything, this unlimited movement that is the temptation of reason, its secret wish, its folly."[7]

Sade's writing to free himself is a gesture of reason, and freedom itself is contingent on it. This saying all, this madness of compulsive writing, is also part of the criminal nature of Sade's texts. Saying everything implies a certain linguistic structure. For Marcel Hénaff:

> This *crime of writing* is of course the one that Sade intends to commit by "saying everything." As an attempt to exhaustively name and stage the signifieds of debauchery, murder and cruelty, "saying everything" produces the writing of obscenity, as a double betrayal of exclusionary rules: the exclusionary rules of communicative language, through the adoption of vulgar words that connote the common people, even (and especially) "the rabble"; and the exclusionary rules of literary language through the radical rejection of metaphorical devices and the convention that upholds them. As a betrayal of class and culture within a generalized corruption of language, "saying everything" is, formally speaking, the crime that engenders all those it enunciates, the Sadean crime par excellence.[8]

Whether corrupter of language, provider of linguistic material normally excluded from language, or blasphemer looking to say what is unspeakable, Sade's attempt at totality in literature and language places him both squarely within his age and before it. The need to encompass knowledge spurred the writers of the Encyclopédie to catalog knowledge. Sade's impulse comes from this Enlightenment desire, but he brings to the surface that which rational minds suppressed. In so doing, he shows the failure of the Enlightenment to encompass all: Sade's texts reveal what many philosophes denied. Perhaps, then, Sade's writing is a "crime" in that it transgresses the boundaries of his age.

The crime of writing is also the mise-en-scène of transgressive eroticism. Writing describes a body. There is an indexical function implicit in this writing that wishes to tell all, to show all: cruelty, reason, and obscenity. Gilles Deleuze states, "In the work of Sade, imperatives and descriptions transcend themselves towards the higher function of demonstration: the demonstrative function is based on universal negativity as an active process, and on universal negation as an Idea of pure reason; it operates by conserving and accelerating the descriptions, which are overlaid with obscenity."[9]

Writing in some ways replaces the body, becomes the body, because only the written word, the corpus, can have the freedom the body once had. Writing about the erotic means saying everything; the body's pleasure is transferred to the page. For Barthes, this transference takes a very specific shape:

> The principle of Sadian eroticism is the saturation of every area of the body: one tries to employ (to occupy) every separate part. This is the same problem the sentence faces (in which respect we have to speak of a Sadian erotography, there being no distinction between the structure of ejaculation and that of language): the (literary, written) sentence is also a body to be catalyzed by filling all its principal sites (subject-verb-complement) with expansions, incidental clauses, subordinates, determinators: of course, this saturation is utopian, for nothing (structurally) permits terminating a sentence: we can always add to it that supplement which will never be the final one.[10]

Wanting to have it all becomes saying it all. This links Sade and Guibert in many ways. Sade's need to bring to the page all his phantoms, to realize his phantoms, means transgressing boundaries of writing, of decency, of rationality. Guibert, too, needs to tell all. He brings the excruciating detail of his sexual phantoms to the reader. In later texts, he gazes so unflinchingly at his own dying body that he, too, transgresses decency and rationality in a writing that must expose all to the core. Perhaps we cannot go as far as Barthes perspicaciously did when discussing Sade's language. Barthes understands Sade's "tout dire" also as a rhetorical strategy, where language itself accumulates semantically and syntactically ad infinitum. Guibert's prose can also be syntactically complex, especially when he is describing encounters with lovers or sexual fantasies. More often Guibert denudes his phrases, refuses himself syntactic indulgences. This sparse prose poignantly punctuates many of his AIDS texts. The rational language of the doctor's office becomes the medium for laying bare the decaying body, for saying all. Sade and Guibert, then, share an unspeakable identity as *dévoileurs,* taking off the veils to expose the hidden truths, although at times they shape language differently to achieve similar ends.

Already in Sade, real prisons he experienced give way to allow writing to take the place of the body. Writing in prison means freeing phantoms to give reign to erotic situations the body can no longer know. Erotic texts written in captivity liberate the body and its impulses. Sade's texts are filled with cloisters, dungeons, closed rooms, torture chambers, and almost every imaginable enclosure to hold victims. Urquhart sees in the boudoir in the text of the same name a veritable theater, a center for theatricality "that qualifies the work, re-presents a scenic space rivaling the holy space of sacrifice."[11] The boudoir in not only the theater but also altar of sacrifice. The enclosure is where one risks it all, to say all.

Sometimes, enclosures lead to self-awareness in Sade; often, young people first experience orgasm and sexual intercourse in a cloister where they were placed by their families or by society. Sean Quinlan goes so far as to assert that, because Sade's ideas can be seen as tributary of the medical knowledge of his day, especially of the interest in hygiene, that the boudoir can become a utopian space as with the hygienic houses of prostitution.[12] More often, the enclosure denies self-identity, as when victims wait in darkened rooms to discover their fate. Very often in Sade, the prison further erodes identity as the body itself begins to lose control of its physical dimensions in an enclosed space. We shall recall the Duc of Blangis's chilling words to his captives on the eve of departure for Silling, where he makes it clear that they have lost all connection to their past. Imprisonment in Silling only seals their fate. Sade's imprisonment produced texts filled with prisons from which he could be liberated by only the most libertine, all-encompassing texts. Guibert, while not himself literally incarcerated, begins to live his own diseased body as a prison. But writing once again provides an escape.

## PRISONS WITHOUT, PRISONS WITHIN

Guibert's intertextual references to his own works and to those of others provide an internal narrative of the intellectual framework that created Guibert the author and the narrator of Guibert's texts, a thinly veiled reference to the author. In *Fou de Vincent*, for example, Guibert mentions other texts he has written—*Les Chiens, Blindsight*—as examples of pornographic textuality, presumably a *mise-en-abyme* reference to the text he is writing. He also mentions Barthes's *A Lover's Discourse*, without admitting that Guibert himself is the presumed object, although he may assume the reader will make the connection. Texts within the text, narrative within the narrative provide a dense web of storytelling that alludes to the story being written. Those internal narratives allow for a writing that says everything, an excess that, as we have seen, is vice for Guibert.

Furthermore, Sarkonak says "at the deepest level, vice exists where there is a prison, one that perhaps does not need walls, as in the case, for example, of the hungry crocodile obligated to give itself in spectacle in front of drunk tourists that watch it eat."[13] Guibert's search for self in his early works connects to his celebrating the homoerotic body. His later works are consumed with Guibert's own body as he comes to terms with the AIDS that wracks it. His work, then, provides in microcosm a view of the shifting nature of AIDS literature as the pandemic expands and grows. Coming to terms with AIDS provides an impetus for the construction and deconstruction of the body in several of Guibert's works as the body becomes a prison from within.

Guibert's literary career parallels almost exactly the chronological progression of the AIDS pandemic. His first novels appeared in 1981, his last were published posthumously in 1992 (several early works from 1977 to 1981 and photographic compilations were published in the early nineties, and his diary pages were published in 2001). Yet his own awareness of AIDS as explored through his texts begins around the time he himself is diagnosed HIV-positive. His earlier works celebrate the body, often the erotic body. In his earliest text, the short story "La Mort propagande," the narrator discovers the body's potential. We will recall that the text begins with a description of the body's theatricality as it stages its own pleasure and pain, and Guibert declares he wants to capture this emotion through his art, whether on film or in a photo. The need to record the body through art—literature, film, and photography—already plays a central role in knowing the body at various stages of development and decay.

The body's erotic freedom continues to be a preeminent theme in Guibert's texts. Guibert published *Les Aventures singulières* in 1982, a collection of short stories that presents vignettes of encounters with a male prostitute in Florence, and of a series of lovers who will appear in later texts. *Les Chiens,* also from 1982, describes an amorous triangle between two men and a woman, as well as many sadomasochistic encounters. The couplings, explicitly described, are equated to the matings of dogs, with their instinctual urges and desires, hence the title. Guibert says he wrote *Les Chiens,* "a sadomasochistic story in the hopes of pleasing [Foucault]."[14] The erotic body becomes the central link between the character, a thinly veiled representation of Guibert himself, and others.

In *Voyage avec deux enfants* (1982) and *Les Lubies d'Arthur* (1983), the body's metaphorical search to experience sexuality with abandon is recounted as fantastic journeys with lovers. In both texts, the theme of voyage not only suggests escape, but also proposes the only escape from the body's captivity and the body's continued enslavement. The title *Voyage avec deux enfants* suggests innocence, even naiveté, but it is a text filled with sexual fantasies about children, the most problematic of sexual phantoms. In this text, one possible escape is through writing: a letter is the ultimate end point of the voyage, the reason for it as well. In *Les Lubies d'Arthur* the voyage metaphor is structured to suggest *Candide,* perhaps even more ominously suggesting Edgar Allan Poe's *Arthur Gordon Pym,* a tragic voyage to the end of the world.[15] In the text, two men travel, but at several turns, they must don disguises. In fact, the theatrical masquerade extends throughout the text: the theater here serves as veritable end point for the voyage. Geneviève Brisac notes, "One finds in *Les Lubies d'Arthur* what made the charm of *Voyage avec deux enfants,* this manner of treating words as things, of collecting them with love, of filling secret drawers with them, to believe in their chemistry."[16] Love, perhaps, for words, but these texts already search for something that risks remaining out of reach, the body of the forbidden Other, a sense of self, the possibility of surviving and leaving a legacy after death.

Guibert is diagnosed HIV-positive in 1988. From this point on, the disease becomes a centering metaphor. The intensity of Guibert's gaze at his own body continues, but now it often reflects a criticism of the body in decay. In *Fou de Vincent,* one of the first texts Guibert wrote with direct references to AIDS, interspersed with allusions to the increasingly evident bodily manifestations of AIDS on Vincent are explicit homoerotic passages in which the narrator celebrates their relationship. In this novel, the narrator/Guibert begins to experience the disease as Other, through the body of the Other. The narrator rarely alludes to the possibility that he himself is at risk. As is often the case with Guibert, however, the reader is confronted with the possible inaccuracy of the text, because in this journal, dates often contradict themselves. What seems autobiographical, a discovery of the self's erotic body, may be "only fiction." *L'Incognito,* also published in 1989, describes a bar where sexual encounters liberate the narrator but also where a mysterious disease looms threateningly in the background.

Published in 1990, *To the Friend Who Did Not Save My Life* chronicles Guibert's realization that he is infected with AIDS. Guibert states that the whole enterprise of writing exists in the realm of failure or of potential failure. "I tell myself that this book's raison d'être lies only along the borderlines of uncertainty, so familiar to all sick people everywhere."[17] In this text, AIDS only exists as its negation, within the boundaries of a possible cure. Guibert traces the spread of AIDS in his friend, Muzil (Michel Foucault) in great detail, as though he were examining the future of his own body in the mirror. Although in this text the self is diseased, it is still reflected through the suffering of the Other.

It begins with a "declaration of sida." The first sentence is "I had AIDS for three months."[18] This text is structured around a failed cure, and on the failure of those around the narrator to help him. Interestingly, even the choice of verb tense in the first sentence implies a hope of being cured. The passé compose tense, "j'ai eu," indicates an event in the past that does not continue, just as the English translation "I had" implies; Guibert almost seems to suggest he is no longer ill. In this text, AIDS only exists as its negation, within the boundaries of a possible cure. Again, although in this text the self is diseased, it is still reflected through the suffering of the Other.

This novel also presents a sort of "history of AIDS" in those who were "the Others" in Guibert's life. The narrator explains how his lovers discovered they were getting ill, when he himself first heard of this "gay plague," and when his friends began to show signs of the disease. In 1980, the bisexual Jules got hepatitis from an Englishman, gave it to the narrator, and almost gave it to his wife. In 1981, Jules became the lover of Ben and Josef in America, at the same time that Bill first mentioned the new disease to the narrator. In December 1981, Jules had sex with Arthur in the presence of the narrator; the Viennese masseur's body was covered with spots and scabs. In 1982, Jules announced the conception of his first child, who was miscarried. In 1982, the narrator allowed an American from Kalamazoo to have sex with him in Budapest. In 1983, Jules had abscesses and enlarged lymph nodes in his throat; 1984 saw the death of Muzil; 1988 was the year the narrator discovered he was ill. He concludes:

> In this chronology summing up and pinpointing the warning signs of the disease over a period of eight years, when we now know that its incubation period is between four and a half and eight years, according to Stéphane, the physiological accidents are no less decisive than the sexual encounters, the premonitions no less telling than the wishes that try to banish them. That's the chronology that becomes my outline, except whenever I discover that progression springs from disorder.[19]

In a sense, this personal chronology of the disease is a way to continue to keep the disease in the realm of the Other. Just as Guibert faces his illness in this novel only from the perspective of a cure, so too does he painstakingly detail the way in which it has affected those around him.

Even the cure comes in the form of the Other: Bill, the mysterious, rich American who promises to enter the narrator in trials of an experimental drug, which he never does. Yet the hope of the cure becomes precisely what the narrator needs to continue writing, which, in the end, is the goal of this last period of his life. For Guibert, AIDS spurs self-discovery. This novel is an assessment of the illness. AIDS represents a way of structuring the work of writing, which will be the path to uncovering the self. It is through AIDS that the narrator finds a reason to continue to write. Writing, in turn, becomes a way to understand the illness in all of its manifestations. The narrator in *Fou de Vincent* surreptitiously came to know the body of his lover and to write about it, to uncover it for himself and for the reader; he undergoes a similar process in *To the Friend Who Did Not Save My Life* with regard to his own body. Bertone has argued for a radical change of perspective regarding this novel with respect to Guibert's previous ones. She notes that already in the title, an ill Guibert loses his power to the "ami." She states that "when the writer's body is contaminated, threatened with destruction due to weakening of the immunological barriers, the corpus of his writing seems likewise displaced, invested as it is by the destruction of the privileged center of observation which had previously allowed it to function as the site of order and control."[20] Perhaps, however, the shift is not as radical as Bertone suggests; Guibert's narrative focuses on the body even in his earlier works. His novels written after he contracted AIDS shift from the body of the Other to the body of the self, but the center of observation remains the *corps.*

It is central, however, to understand the focus on Foucault's dying body in this context. Much has been made of the barely veiled reference to Foucault in this text. The philosopher died of AIDS in 1984. The official hospital bulletin released on Foucault's death lists the cause as neurological manifestations that complicated a septicemic state. The day after, *Libération* published an unsigned article denouncing the rumors that Foucault died of AIDS, as though in his role as intellectual, he were being made to die a shameful death. Guibert published *Mauve le vierge* in 1988 as a first salvo in his war against what he perceives as the hypocrisy surrounding Foucault's death. In the text "Les Secrets d'un

homme" included in the volume, a man whose great mind the
doctor cannot bear to autopsy dies of leprosy. In this text, Guibert muses about the nature of the human mind and its relationship to the persona of the dead individual. This reflection is
certainly similar to the types of issues Guibert faces and the rea-
sons why writing and AIDS are intertwined in his work. With that
text, and more so with *To the Friend Who Did Not Save My Life*
and its character Muzil, Guibert divides intellectuals into two
camps in the argument on revealing secrets. In essence, he forces
a debate on the limits of literature, on whether it is possible to
say everything.[21] Buot affirms, "In the debate, Hervé's response
is not to plead to justify himself. Not an argument, but a cry: you
will not impede me from writing all, from saying all. In the fight
against illness, truth is required, writing is required, to save oneself."[22] Caron, in a passage cited in a previous chapter, noted that
in Guibert gossip provides queer readers with a familiar mode of
communication.[23] The hidden speech act revealed becomes a
way to say everything.

Guibert is adamant about looking at this disease as he had all
other aspects of his relationship to his body: without blinking. Although some criticized Guibert for unveiling the nature of Foucault's disease against the philosopher's wishes, doing so is
consistent with Guibert's approach to AIDS. Guibert identifies
with the great thinker *as* thinker, not only as gay, diseased Other,
which is often his relationship to other friends who are HIV-positive. Foucault remains whole through his texts, as Guibert obviously hopes to do. The act of writing itself holds out hope for the
cure. In this novel, Guibert writes about the hope of a cure, and
the cure comes through writing itself.

Guibert's illness creates a new mask for him in some ways, a
new identity he must negotiate. In *To the Friend Who Did Not
Save My Life,* his illness is a secret he can leave behind when he
goes to Rome. Yet he must reveal his new identity to a former
lover, for one, who may have been infected. Guibert "let the truth
slip out,"[24] as though dropping a mask before the one who might
share his identity. Guibert advises his former lover, Matou, whose
girlfriend is three months pregnant, to take the HIV test. As they
walk, Guibert asks Matou about the test results. It is almost a moment of cruelty, "It was a difficult moment, an instant in which
one might think that the other had doubts about the real open-

ness of one's heart."[25] This prurient concern recalls the barbarous delicacy that, for Guibert, links his work to Sade's. Illness, a new identity, becomes a transcendent link to the past. It also becomes a subtle form of torture, where the victimizer waits as the possible victim lives the anguish of not knowing whether he, too, will have to assume a new identity.

Furthermore, with the character of Muzil representing a writer whose works were so influential, Guibert insists in this text on assuming another identity: that of his dead friend. Both writer and fellow AIDS victim, Muzil represents the nexus where new identity, multiple identities, converge. In *To the Friend Who Did Not Save My Life,* Bill does not save the narrator's life by failing to provide medications, but Muzil also does not save his life. Muzil renders him vulnerable to the multiplication of identities.

AIDS novels follow in rapid succession, as Guibert works feverishly to recount his life. Increasingly, too, the virus's effect on his body distances him from its materiality. The body becomes estranged, ever more trapping him inside its progressive decay. In *The Compassion Protocol,* he recalls his attempts to be included in the trials of an experimental drug. He wishes to be among the first survivors of the disease. Guibert himself states that, while *To the Friend Who Did Not Save My Life* involved a "coming to terms with the illness and its work on body and soul, *The Compassion Protocol* chronicles my astonishment and misery, my rage and the grief of a man of thirty-five on whom is grafted the body of an old man. But the happiness of remission makes an inroad into the unhappiness."[26]

This is a novel of fatigue and decay. The effect AIDS has on the narrator—how it slows him down and how those around him begin to notice the aging process in him—becomes a central theme of this work. A passage describes how the body is subjected to an endoscopy, to the constant prodding of doctors. There is virtually no escape through love and tenderness in the novel, since sexuality has virtually ceased. The narrator feels as though he were a pig at slaughter, whose body no longer belongs to him. The body in this novel may be feeling more alive thanks to new medication, but it is also slipping away from the narrator. But this is also the novel in which he videotapes his doctors and others in a feverish attempt to record everything. While disease ravages the body, artistic production reclaims the self. In this text, as the body weakens, medicalization of disease and medicines are the central focus.

Grasping at the vestiges of identity through art becomes an obsession as also seen in the paintings the narrator wants to acquire:

> The collecting of pictures, that fever that mounts when making choices, that sudden enthusiasm turning to doubt, the discussion of a price, the pleasure of seeing how a work fits in with or clashes with the other paintings I possess, this solitary and feverish activity that makes me race from one dealer to another in Paris or Rome, entering with one or the other into a relationship I find very special and passionate in pursuit of our desires, I to possess, he or she to know the joy of finally getting rid of some daub; with my flag of erotic activity at half mast, the purchase of paintings is also a substitute for sensuality and a sexual presence, for I still insist on living alone, however much they warn me, both doctors and intimates, that it's inadvisable now: a painting radiates a familiar and almost physical presence throughout my apartment, I'd even say that this corporal expression of phantoms radiating from my pictures, and so too the collection of art, encourages and fosters this illusion that I shall go on living.[27]

This text sees the body losing its sexual identity as it decays. It becomes more difficult to reach sexual satisfaction, to find partners, because the focus has moved inward toward survival. Writing and art have also become substitutes for sexual identity. Buying pictures becomes a substitute for sexuality, a theme that continues in Guibert's works as he pushes desperately to write until the end.

*The Man in the Red Hat* again describes Guibert's developing symptoms of the disease. He now knows that there are no miracle cures for him, only procedures to ward off opportunistic infections as they take hold. He merely wishes to maintain his dignity. The red hat, and hats in general, represent this dignity for Guibert. In fact, the hat, which can conceal his hair loss due to illness, allows the patient to reclaim an aesthetic relationship to his body. This novel weaves a plot about the search for artistic fakes, paintings in particular, into the parallel story of the narrator's disease progression. The art-forgery subplot reminds us that in Guibert, the construction of the body and its deconstruction parallel a dubious authenticity of his literary works. One is never quite sure if they are real or not.

*Cytomegalovirus: A Hospitalization Diary* (1992) brings together the threads of Guibert's works and represents a culmination of the AIDS theme. Guibert had stated in *The Compassion Protocol* that "It is when what I am writing takes the form of a journal that I most strongly feel that I am writing fiction."[28] The reader could very easily be led to take *Cytomegalovirus: A Hospitalization Diary* as pure "autobiography," unlike the quasiautobiographical style in which virtually all of Guibert's production is written. Yet his statement in *The Compassion Protocol* indicates that no text is real for Guibert. Even those texts whose genre would have us believe they detail real events must be read as text, as symbol, as Other. In this, the very act of writing involves moving beyond oneself, into the realm of the Other, the diary format perhaps more so than most other genres, because it violates the reader's expectations of fiction. Guibert plays with genre to create a text that is all the more compelling for its stark qualities.

Among other aspects, this startling journal is a work of resistance. Guibert fights to maintain the dignity of his body and the wholeness of it, despite the dehumanizing medical environment. Caron traces this redemption of self in the face of medical impersonality, even cruelty, in several of Guibert's works. In *Cytomegalovirus: A Hospitalization Diary*, Caron notes, "Resistance takes the simple and immediate form of symbolic acts, as . . . when Guibert refuses to wear '[t]he transparent blue gown [which] had no purpose other than humiliation.'"[29] Guibert walks to the operating room wearing the green gown the doctors wear. Caron again states that "[S]uch an act, the appropriation and resignification of the doctor's clothes, constitutes in itself an act of resistance insofar as it re-creates the symbolic construction of the 'doctor' and, implicitly, of the 'patient.' By repeating and imitating such a construction, he de-naturalizes these two categories, and directly confronts the power relationship that governs them."[30] As Butler might suggest, body identity and power are dependent on one another. In *Cytomegalovirus: A Hospitalization Diary*, Guibert has abandoned the hopeless search for a cure. He concentrates instead on maintaining his wholeness of spirit in the face of a failing body.

While Guibert reclaims the body through writing, he also rediscovers the erotic body that he had progressively lost, as we have seen in the previous texts that recount his struggle with AIDS. Toward the end of the novel, Guibert sees a man on a gurney in the hospital ward, and the sight of the body excites him. "When I rediscover an erotic emotion, it's a little bit of life that I discover in this death bath."[31] Yet Guibert believes sexuality is impossible when he learns that the antiviral DHPG (gancyclovir) they have been perfusing into his veins daily irreversibly blocks the production of sperm. He stoically concludes, "But I don't give a fuck about fucking now."[32] This final denial of physical love does not preclude emotional attachment or erotic yearnings, which have been revived. The erotic body remains the locus of the self until the end, but the physical possibilities of love are consummated in writing.

The body itself is failing, however, notably the eyes, as Guibert fights cytomegalovirus. Sight is privileged in fact in Guibert's work. As Brault has observed, Guibert's works are not only obsessed with the body, but also with vision:

> Guibert left us a collection of books which structure the double consideration of the body and the gaze as it exists in the tension between autobiography and fiction. Guibert speaks incessantly of the body, page after page; the body, his or that of the Other, eroticized to the extreme, animated at times by the most perverse instincts, initiator of the most obsessional attractions, yet also source of repulsion, a warning sign of inevitable rotting and death. This body, whether autobiographical or fictional, is created by sight, which guides it through the passions of the one who sees or does not see, the lover or the photographer, the patient or the blind person.[33]

In *Cytomegalovirus: A Hospitalization Diary*, Guibert himself notes that blindness and sight have been obsessions for him throughout his literary production. One of his earlier works, *Ghost Image*, is a text without pictures that discusses photography. In a sense, it attempts to "see" photography in a way that a blind person could also see it. This text discusses photography from a very technical, but also a very personal angle. It reads at times like a treatise on the art form, although in reality it is Guibert's musing on his own attraction to that art. A later work, *Vice*, intersperses photos with descriptions that do not explicate the photos. The images in this text present odd moments from a walk in a museum after hours, with mannequins piled in corners, and other strange objects. The texts, on the other hand, are minute descriptions of the most ordinary objects, such as cotton swabs, scalpels, and threads, which are not figured in the pictures juxtaposed to them. "Vice," according to the author, is this casual blending of disparate elements and reveling in the close analysis of the banal, a very Sadean reflection. In *Vice,* Guibert holds a position opposite to that in *Ghost Image:* only those who are sighted can comprehend the photos, since descriptions of them are flawed.

In between these two texts, Guibert wrote *Blindsight,* a novel in which the blind play a prominent role. Guibert appears in the novel as a sighted person among the blind interned in a state home. But in the end, we as readers are presented with several narrators, several narrations, and perhaps some narrators who are sighted and some who are blind. We must navigate this text as though we, too, were blind, unable to recognize the one and only narrator. We learn that Guibert indeed spent several months reading to the blind in this institution. The interaction of the senses, the loss of one of the senses, and the implications of this on those with an intact sensory system are explored in this novel. In *Cytomegalovirus: A Hospitalization Diary,* Guibert notes the irony of his fascination with blindness now that he risks going blind. For a photographer such as Guibert, the gaze signifies. Blindness, absence of gaze, represents absence of art, absence of life. The incomplete body, which adds interest to a subject for art, now becomes his life, the diseased body that creates the art of the text.

In *Cytomegalovirus: A Hospitalization Diary,* Guibert now realizes that for him, it is not only that "the eye is at stake," but the possibility of transferring the experience of it all onto paper. He asks himself in the last lines, "Writing in the dark? Writing until the end? To end it so as not to end up fearing death?"[34] In other words, he asks if life and writing can truly coincide. This is the project that he had hoped to complete. His works focus on the body as it discovers and glorifies its sexuality. When the body becomes diseased, it continues to be scrutinized, flaws and all. Imperfections become marks of telling. In the last phase of his career, writing becomes the continuation of life, the life-source.

Guibert makes it clear he wishes life and writing to coincide completely, ideally writing until the very last.

He almost succeeds. *Paradise* (1992) was produced during the last months of his life. In this text, paradise is a voyage to an exotic location, Bora Bora. The three voyagers turn out to be friends and their encounter takes on sexual overtones: The orgy is a moment of contact. As was the case in *Les Chiens* and in Sade's texts, the scene is recounted from different points of view. The actors are also spectators, for the erotic is both within the characters and outside of them. The body is in a sense imprisoned in the erotic. In a final scene of fecundation in *Paradise*, the reader sees this as more than brutality, again as was the case for *Les Chiens*.

Sade's imprisonment led to the liberating possibilities of writing. His sexual identity was not allowed free reign, but the sexual phantoms generated through denial brought about the texts replete with sexual excess. A new identity, in some sense, of writer was born through repression of sexuality. In a corpus of works filled with prisons that further erode the body's sense of identity, Sade creates a universe where the body begins to lose corporeality as it waits for torture or death. Many of Guibert's texts also have prisons of one kind or another: the cave in *Vous m'avez fait former des fantômes*, the institute for the blind in *Blindsight*, his family home in *My Parents* or *Ghost Image*, and the hospital in *To the Friend Who Did Not Save My Life*, *The Compassion Protocol*, and *Cytomegalovirus: A Hospitalization Diary*, to name only a few. Still, for Guibert, the body becomes his primary prison. It becomes trapped within itself, a prison of accelerated decay. The possibility of giving freedom to the sexual identity so celebrated in earlier texts becomes limited as the body strives to survive. Writing itself becomes the substitute for sexuality, the way to stay alive. Even in his last texts, for Guibert, the body is chained by constraints, although it seeks freedom through voyage. Writing takes the place of liberation and sexuality because writing is motivated by and enacted when physical freedom and sexuality are no longer possible. However, this threatens to turn writing into a kind of imprisonment in a postmodern way. It takes the place of and in some ways compensates for physical loss of freedom. But then writing is necessary and present only when "real" freedom has disappeared. In the end, the only freedom comes with writing about the search for freedom.

# 5

## Disappearing Act: Bodies
## Dissected, Ghostly Remains

IN BOTH SADE'S AND GUIBERT'S TEXTS, MANY OF THE PERVERSIONS FOCUS on fragmenting the body. As the tortures continue throughout the 120 days in Sade, for example, victims are subjected to physical lacerations of the flesh, and at the end, dismemberment becomes the ultimate punishment. In Sade, bodies are cut to pieces. Victims bring their bodies to the theater where sexual perversions play out, and the tortures eventually lead to death. The medical image of the dissecting table comes to mind. The anatomy theater is where bodies are methodically disassembled to expose the intimate spaces they contain, and in the case of medical autopsy, perhaps to bring to light diseases. In Sade as well, the body's inner workings are what interests the torturers. Sexual pleasure can no longer come from copulation with a whole body. Only the fragments of bodies continue to arouse. The sexual object is fetishistically dismantled as the ultimate sexual thrill. And having the power to cut a body into inhuman parts is the ultimate aphrodisiac.

This vision of the body in pieces as the result of the sexual act could be tied to the political climate in which Sade lived. *The 120 Days of Sodom* begins with an evocation of the corruption of the end of Louis XIV's reign, several decades before Sade was born. The four friends who organize the castle rendezvous all are said to have benefited from graft and bribes common during this period. In a description quite accurate in its economic acumen, *The 120 Days of Sodom* begins by declaring that, although the considerable wars Louis XIV fought depleted the State's finances and the people's resolve, they were able to enrich a great quantity of bloodsuckers always rife during times of public calamity. The Duc of Blangis, for example, took full advantage of this potential

107

for enrichment.[1] The narrator continues to emphasize their immense wealth which they pool to create the elaborate, extravagant cruelties they inflict on their victims. Their unlimited wealth
leads them to invent the pleasures of the flesh played out in the
novel. The power invested in the nobility during the time evoked
in Sade's novel was unlimited, so by extension, noblemen perpetuate unlimited suffering on others. Just as the lower classes
suffered abuse, physical and otherwise, at the hands of the ruling
classes, the Duc of Blangis and his entourage subjugate nameless
victims for sexual gratification.

If we recall the first pages of Foucault's *Discipline and Punishment*, he shows that extreme punishments under the Ancien Régime involved not only death, but also complete annihilation of
the body of the victim. In describing the execution of the attempted regicide of Louis XV, Damiens in 1757, Foucault notes
the uselessness of most of the methods of execution. Long after
the man was dead, his body was torn to pieces and much more,
all to prove, according to Foucault, that the king held ultimate
power over the body of each of his subjects. Bodies belonged to
the one holding absolute power.[2] In that same way, the sexual
machinations of the four friends are inscribed entirely in a political stance of complete control over the victims. Dismemberment
is necessary to prove that control.

For Guibert, dismemberment is less literal, evident in several
of his texts as well as in his photographs. In several series of photos taken in the archives of museums, Guibert shows mannequin
parts, sometimes stacked in piles so it seems like the aftermath
of a dismemberment. Disjointed bodies lack specificity, and
through several of his photos, Guibert shows the lonely, frightening monotony of the human body when it is reduced to its component parts and thus devoid of identity and wholeness.
Ultimately, however, even the parts of bodies that litter the text
disintegrate. In Guibert, the body disappears leaving only a
phantom image. This image trace is discernible in several of
Guibert's texts. The photograph, especially, proves an ideal genre
for revealing ghostly images, and Guibert's photos cause shadows; they allude without revealing, as though they had captured
something beyond the corporeal. For Sade and Guibert, taking
control over bodies continues the disarticulation of the body
from its identity, from time, and from space.

## Dissecting Bodies

In Sade, Lucienne Frappier-Mazur notes, "There is no break in continuity between the dismembering of the body and organ pleasure, on the one hand, and numerical organization on the other. The obsession with numbers and classification, which originates in anality, is linked to coprophiliac obsession, and heterogeneous elements are replicated by serial schemata." She continues that fragmentation of the body serves to create equivalences and to level everything, "Somewhat akin to La Mettrie's Machine-Man, the Sadean machine serves to suppress all transcendental agency, to deny interiority, and to ensure the anonymity of the erotic group, without excluding the voluntarist stance of the Sadean libertine."[3]

We have seen Sade's obsession with numbers, especially in *The 120 Days of Sodom*, as a way of controlling time and providing another avenue of torture for the victims. In a more psychoanalytic reading, this obsession is, like others, linked to formation arrested at the anal stage. Frappier-Mazur suggests that fragmentation sustains the mechanical aspects of Sade's works. Loss of identity, mechanization of the object of desire, and the fragmented body allow for both political and sexual control. We have seen that machines begin to take over the role of torturer as the months progress at Château Silling. As sexual intercourse becomes increasingly mechanized, participants continue to play roles, perhaps themselves like a machine in operation. Whether discussing the individual machines invented as tortures, the group dynamics of loss of body and identity, or the mechanization of the sex act, the body's fragmentation is both side effect and cause of this process. Along with the mechanical aspects of dismemberment by an inhuman process that treats the body like a machine, the medical metaphor surfaces when discussing dismemberment as a clinical act. The dissecting table image appears in many texts. Quinlan's study of *Philosophy in the Boudoir* analyzes Saint-Ange's mirrored boudoir where the protagonists take turns on the ottoman couch playing the cadaver "like an anatomist dissecting in a surgical amphitheater."[4] He notes several times that Sade's texts are tributary of the medical practices of the day, so this correlation of dismemberment and dissection goes hand in hand.

We can understand the sacrifice of bodies in Sade as part of an economy of form. The materiality of the body is progressively threatened as the structure of the space around it becomes more rigid. The exchange value of the body is minimal because one victim can easily substitute for another. Anal intercourse being privileged in this Sadean universe, bodies can easily stand in for one another. The storytellers, thanks to their function as recorders of deeds, as it were, are assigned some value. The cooks are even spared, and therefore are the most prized commodity in Silling because they provide a unique service for the inhabitants. The victims, however, "good for" only one thing—satisfying the increasingly insatiable sexual appetites of the four friends—are really only a disconnected series of body parts. Whole bodies have little value; body cavities have value, but one can substitute for another. So in Sade, in one sense, the victims' bodies are economically worthless. At the end of *The 120 Days of Sodom*, March 1, the narrator provides a ledger sheet, a veritable invoice written with a column of numbers to the right, of those murdered and those spared. Although only ten were killed previous to March 1, victims of ritual murders, twenty must be killed immediately before returning to Paris. Only sixteen remain according to the text.[5] One invoice shows those who were originally in the castle by category (for example fuckers and wives) Another shows the "balance of massacres" (before and after March 1). Despite the already accelerated and abbreviated format for the second, third, and fourth parts of the text, the extreme numeration and objectification of victims bring their dehumanization to its supreme conclusion.

What of the bodies of the four friends? They are of course valued from the onset of the text because they represent the last vestiges of the Ancien Régime's absolute power. Money is of prime importance in the text because it provides for the limitless food and sexual excesses of the group. For Frappier-Mazur, "It comes as no surprise that money is an ordering principle for the orgy. As a closed system, money was bound to fascinate Sade. Understood as both the means to sexual pleasure and its symbol, money shares the ritual character of orgy and possesses semimagical qualities."[6] David Martyn discusses economics in ethical terms, relating it to Kant or Adam Smith. He understands Sade's texts as Smithian "economics."[7] When the four friends embark on their pleasure trip, their only concern is organizing the time, space, and actors so as to maximize their own sexual gratification. Bored with their usual sexual practices in France and with their already seemingly endless sexual partners—having violated even the incest taboo, for example—only the carefully crafted architecture of a sexual vacation will satisfy them. The orgy is dependent on money, which brings with it also social, political, and sexual power.

Within this economy of sexual exchange, the victims' bodies themselves paradoxically have virtually no value but are quite valuable. The victims were specially selected, they are fed to keep them alive to endure tortures, but their bodies are subjected to tortures that ultimately kill them. Were they to escape, the scenarios so carefully erected by the four friends would be undermined. So the victims' value may lie in their expendability. It is their anonymity that makes them interesting as victims. By bringing them to the castle outside France, the friends know they can perpetrate their fantasies on these bodies without risk of legal retributions. Anonymous, taken from the people they know who might report them missing,[8] and stripped of identities, the Silling victims are ideal sexual slaves. The torturers can allow their phantoms complete freedom. This very anonymity also makes the victims completely expendable. In fact, the fragmentation of the body, dissolution, is the ultimate fantasy. Dissection is the first phase of the complete control that brings complete sexual fulfillment.

In some of Guibert's photos, whole bodies seem to float freely but their composition and juxtaposition denote a disturbing lack of intimacy. *Vice* includes several photos that make allusion to theatrical staging by showing figures, usually mannequins, flying from pulleys on the ceiling of an abandoned space such as a museum by night or a taxidermist's shop. These illustrations denote an almost desperate attempt to fly. These photos seem to elicit a sense of pathos for the impossibility of leaving the weight of the earth.

In these instances, however, there is no suggestion of sexuality. For Guibert, the bodies seem to want to defy gravity. In the end, vice is like desire, a lack waiting to be filled, to be satisfied. For Pierre Saint-Amand, "photography for Guibert is always a cry not only for light but for desire. It is always on stage. It enters always into the syntactic articulation of the phantom."[9] Vice alludes to sexual gratification, to desire, but seems doomed to bring on only phantoms. The figures, perhaps like the author himself, are trying to move beyond the body, to become weightless, as he struggles to come to terms with the disappearance of the body.

Fragmentation of bodies abounds in these photos, too. Like Guibert's texts, which include scenes of characters killed and maimed, often for the sexual gratification of others or at least as a result of violence in sexually charged situations, these body parts prove disquieting. Sexual identity also comes into play. Several photos demonstrate the ways in which the body under Guibert's camera eye fragments. In *Vice*, especially, many photos also place figures into elaborate architectural frames: in doorways, on tables, arranged neatly before the viewer. This multiplication of detached parts provides an excess leading toward the grotesque, as though these limbs were leftovers from a massacre. Their neat arrangement on tables, in trays, and so forth, however, gives a paradoxical rationality to this disorder.

In some ways, Guibert's images of dismembered bodies are less rational than Sade's, as evidenced by the textual descriptions in the marquis's texts, where the orgiastic bodies seemed constructed. In Sade, it was the coupling of bodies that created a geometric space to conspire with the geometrical obsession of dates, times, and rituals in the texts. In Guibert, the bodies flying through the air, the lifeless beings, and the dismembered body parts do not couple. The figures and members follow one another or are juxtaposed in the same frame but do not touch or respond to one another. In fact, human contact here is not even suggested. This difference marks a variation between Sade's "vice" and Guibert's. For the former, the individual body loses its singularity and only the sexual act, the body linked to another body, can bring about sexual pleasure, can be attributive of vice. For the latter, instead, the body in isolation, the solitude and the crushing weight of losing contact with others, is vice, and the exquisite pain and pleasure that arouses.

Alienation and despair come through in several of Guibert's photos that suggest dissection. Some photos focus more clearly on mannequin parts, for example. Again in *Vice*, in photos of lifeless bodies, the issue of dissection comes most into focus. In some photos, the scene has been arranged like a dissection table, with a head and a hand visible. The props on which they are placed (tables, chairs, and so forth) and the absence of medical equipment leads us to see this grouping as a literal theater rather than an anatomical one. Some photos with the title "self portrait" even hearken back to Guibert's notions of the body as theater for the erotic as studied in previous chapters. The body is still "staged," still cut for the viewer who will not allow it to remain whole.

We know that for Guibert, one of the ways of moving back from the abyss is the possibility of leaving something behind, of writing in the dark, of writing until the end so that the text leaves a trace of the body, a phantom. Some of Guibert's photos instead suggest that communication is not possible. The solitude so devastating for the body has no escape. In some photos, dismembered heads have an unreal quality. They seem to face one another attempting to talk, but they have no facial features; they seem lifeless. Often, in photographs using backlighting, the light behind the figures gives an otherworldly glow to the scene. The heads here search but cannot find one another. They are all mute. There is a lack of communication, a linguistic imprisonment that echoes physical imprisonment. At times for Guibert, writing and interacting may be the answer, but at other times, nothing remains. Vice is the illusion of superfluity, of excess, of fragmentation, and the multiplication of body parts gives that illusion.

This is in contrast to Guibert's other photographic texts collected during his lifetime. In *Dialogue d'Images* (Dialogue of Images), for example, or in the compilation of his works, *Photographies* (Photographs), published posthumously, Guibert portrays friends in various locations and poses. These are texts largely of portraits, with many self-portraits as well. Guibert has faces look directly at the viewer, has them stare at us as we stare back at them. The voyeur is now under observation, akin to the gaze of Kahlo's self-portraits. In *Vice*, however, the photographic record of wanderings through empty spaces populated only by the remains of lifeless bodies (such as animals embalmed, mannequin body parts waiting for assembly, and mannequins suspended from ceiling waiting to be shipped to new venues), bodies come apart. Mannequin hands may be poised as though in anguish next to a head, but the figures are only simulations of bodies.

In some self-portraits, however, only a hand reaches out, away from the body. The camera focuses on the outstretched hand as it would the face in a portrait. The fingers flex, almost defiantly, but they have nothing to hold on to except air. In some ways, this is like the self-portrait as genre; the fingers' reaching for each other is a self-reflexive gesture, an essentially lonely one. Guibert's photos often suggest a fragmentation that goes beyond mere photographic curiosity. By showing inanimate, humanlike creations in pieces, Guibert shows the body at its most vulnerable. Loss of identity, anonymity, leads to bodies losing their materiality as well. The positioning of multiple parts together—groups of mannequin hands and mannequin heads and other body parts on tables—provides ironic commentary on the anonymity already suggested by the use of mannequins as subjects. Parts are interchangeable, an idea suggested in Sade.

In Guibert, however, this idea is less linked to an economy of exchange where victims are expendable. There is a fundamental loneliness in Guibert's photos behind the uneasiness created by this series of detached members. Murray Pratt understands Guibert's isolation as an effect of his position to his own sexuality:

> Hervé Guibert, far from being suffocated by the oppressions institutionalized by autobiography and homophobia as Sedgwick describes it instead tries to rise to the challenge they posed. The various incognitos, pseudonyms and reinventions of self that run through his work represent in fact a series of attempts to put aside the nefarious identity of the homosexual, a term Guibert chooses to consider off limits, but that still signifies each of the identifications he invents in order to destabilize the taboos of homophobia.[10]

Pratt refers to Sedgwick's ideas of the closet as enclosed, defining space, as we discussed with the exploration of Goffman and stigmatized identity in a previous chapter. Several critics mention, as does Pratt, that Guibert is not a writer who discusses homosexuality as a construct to combat homophobia in a political way. But Pratt rightly points out that the loss of identity through many strategies and in many textual contexts allows

Guibert to destabilize taboos. The loneliness implicit in some of his photos corresponds to the decentered identity of his characters that probably relates to an understanding of gay sexuality as it relates to heterosexuality. Sexuality, desire, alienation, loss of identity, and disappearance come into focus under Guibert's camera lens.

The photos contained in *Lettres d'Egypte,* one of the texts published posthumously, also allude to this loneliness. In the picture's background we often see an Egyptian monument, a ruin, or a country landscape, while hidden among the ruins appears a tiny human figure watching the photographer—and the spectator—through his lens. Egypt as a location seems particularly revealing as well, for Guibert explores with special care and detail monuments associated with death. Egypt, a land where a cult of the dead structured society, provides a particularly nourishing landscape of loneliness where history's timelessness overwhelms the individual.

Written as a series of letters, the work should have a connectedness that is somehow lacking. Through descriptions of sights and sounds of the new land as befits a travelogue, Guibert intersperses reminiscences to his friends with strikingly personal details. And yet the photographs that create rhythms in the text show solitary statues of Egyptian figures in temple corners, Guibert alone on a stairwell gazing out an open window, and empty tables and chairs in a wooded garden. These letters reach out to those he knows and try to connect with new experiences, but fundamentally the narrator is alone. Through photography, the emptiness of the ghost landscape appears.

Perhaps for Guibert, the body, as it begins to show its impending vulnerability, cannot remain whole. One of his texts before discovering his seropositivity, *L'Homme blessé,* may be a metaphor for Guibert's work. The body is wounded and disappears in the night without a trace. As he watches his body succumb to the disease, he focuses on parts of the body that work differently because they are ill or that seem to have become older, much too old for the body of a man in his early thirties. In his visual works, dismemberment suggests abandonment, the loss of individuality, and the body's ultimate disappearance.

## DISINTEGRATING BODIES

The theme of destruction, of destroying that which is carefully crafted, underlies both Sade and Guibert. For Guibert especially, the body is destroyed through disease. The body becomes a traitor to the self. Although it had been the center of the recreation of the self as gay man in sexual encounters, the body after AIDS lets Guibert down at various junctures. Writing will be the only salvation from total destruction.

For destruction is inevitable, as Steven F. Kruger has written, "AIDS, after all, is constructed as an illness that, in affecting immunity, challenges the body's 'defenses' and thus radically alters its relation to the threatening realm of 'not-self' that the immune system properly 'polices.' The intact 'fortress' of the body is weakened, made susceptible to 'attack' and 'invasion.' "[11] Emphasizing the military metaphors often used to describe disease processes, a rhetorical strategy explored to great effect in Susan Sontag's works on disease, Kruger shows how this military conflict of the body against itself contributes to loss of identity.

This viral assault on the body affects writing. For Bertone, as we have noted, when the body becomes contaminated, writing is in danger.[12] Loss of identity, Bertone rightly surmises, imperils writing itself, and we know that for Guibert, leaving a literary trace behind represents the only possibility of reversing annihilation. Even more, the writing produced after the body is infected changes. For Buot,

> The diagnosis of illness that marks the body brings with it also a radical change in the writer's work. The virus' progression paradoxically feeds the desire to multiply and diversify the work. . . . Hervé is confronted with a dizzying shortening of his life. He has to write quickly, fight against fatigue, and try to obtain a stay of execution for the body and for writing. Simply put, with his public avowal of illness, the countdown seems to accelerate. He has to act fast! AIDS becomes Hervé's "work." [13]

AIDS itself, then, is perhaps the writing of Guibert's last years. Illness has supplanted the body as subject because it forced the body to begin disappearing. Writing is dependent on AIDS, and

AIDS becomes the focus of the writing project. In an exchange between the body and the text, AIDS is the catalyst that binds them but remains unchanged. In exploring *The Compassion Protocol*, Isabelle Décarie says, "If transfusion-writing and the immediacy of retranscription translate a new stage of the illness, they are also linked to the singular state of the narrator's body."[14] We could reach this conclusion in all of Guibert's works on fragmented bodies. In what Décarie calls his transfusion-writing, Guibert substitutes the body of work for the body. Fragmentation accelerates the disintegration of bodies, just as his own body fragments. In the texts and in his photos, the work glorifies the breaking apart but the work itself holds the pieces together.

## Phantom Bodies / Phantom Images

In both authors, phantoms, mirages, and incognitos lurk behind the veneer of the fictional space, pointing to that space and alluding to the inevitability of death. In the works of a writer embedded in the philosophies of a century enamored with rational discourse, it is not surprising that supernatural elements are somewhat rare in Sade's texts. Divine intervention sometimes plays a role, but primarily as a way to show its arbitrary nature as a way of negating divinity itself, as in the bolt of lightning having the final say in a life of torments survived. Still, in *The 120 Days of Sodom*, the company and the narrative dissipate and leave only numerical order (after all, the last pages of the text contain ledger sheets of who was killed, when, and how). The marquis ends his tale by enjoining readers to fill in the gaps of the last suffering characters on our own, even inventing our own tortures for them. The characters themselves disappear and leave only the phantoms created in the reader's mind to finish out the story.

In Sade, liberty is a mirage always present in the shadows tantalizing the victims who, like Tantalus, can never reach their goal. In the speech the Duc of Blangis delivers to the friends and victims assembled the night before the departure of the merry band for the castle, he tells the captives unequivocally that escape will be impossible for them. He declares that at Silling, and in its dense surrounding forest, only death abounds everywhere. Death is ever present in the sexual rituals of the four friends. Each of them is allowed to set the theme and tone for one of the four months. The themes grow increasingly menacing, until the fourth month's activities all revolve around the death of the sexual victims. Delon has rightly pointed out that the decreasing level of detail in relating the daily activities of each of the four months recounted in *The 120 Days of Sodom* (there is less detail in the narration of events during the fourth month than during the first)[15] hints at the impossibility of writing the unspeakable. Murder as an inevitable consequence of the sex act—the inexorable link between *eros* and *thanatos* in the fourth month, renders the writer mute. Death, lurking in the shadows of the text as punishment for disobeying sexual orders, now overwhelms the text as sexuality becomes death.

What takes shape after the body's disintegration is the phantom image, formed from desire. We recall that, for Lacan, pleasure and desire are linked in a phantom image. Phantoms lead to pleasure because they are distinct from the subject. They are the infinitely unattainable, just as without desire there is only death. Desire becomes not only a sign of life but life itself. Yet desire, the nonsubject, exists as the antithesis to the subject and its concreteness. It exists in the realm of ghosts.[16]

Disappearance and phantom images begin to appear early in Guibert's fiction. Both characters and author begin to play hide-and-seek with the reader early on. In *Les Lubies d'Arthur,* Guibert disappears for the first time in his fiction.[17] This text presents a theme Guibert returned to several times in early texts, especially a voyage with two children filled with fantastic adventures.

> But as is always the case with Hervé, the paradise of childhood adventures is not a rose garden. There is also a good dose of immodesty, of passions, of savagery, of spit and of blood . . . the two friends indulge in sex, murder, and robbery, and they are both victim and executioner. Moreover, death hovers near, and despite Arthur's words of love, Bichon goes away forever . . . the world becomes heavy, hard, and Arthur resists as best he can by going to cemeteries to clasp the dead.[18]

Childhood in Guibert rarely proves a period of innocence or carefree abandon. His own childhood as recounted in *My Parents,* for example, was difficult and lonely. In his other fictions,

children are exposed to adult dangers or even dangers perpetrated by adults on them. Children's bodies, in a way, their identities, immediately become adult. Like Guibert himself, children
in his fiction become old before their time. Pratt notes phantasmagoric departures of seducers in Guibert's text *Voyage avec
deux enfants,* part of an ambiguous strategy of otherness.[19] Even
in *Voyage avec deux enfants*, seduction, intimacy, and corporeal
instability mark a strategy of ambiguous otherness. In text after
text, sexuality leads to instability and to corporeal dissolution.

Guibert's bodily disappearance culminates in a ghost image:
textual, photographic, or cinematic. When exploring Guibert's
land of ghosts and his relationship with Sade, the most important
text remains *Vous m'avez fait former des fantômes,* according to
Sarkonak the least well known of Guibert's works[20] and a crucial
text to understanding phantoms in Guibert. Bruno Blanckeman
explains part of the title of *Vous m'avez fait former des fantômes:*
Guibert adopts some of the strategies of the marquis, that is, the
idea of delicateness of discourse. "The more the proposal is hu-
manly untenable, the more the tenor of the rhetoric imposes itself."[21] In many ways, this is a key text. It straddles the years when
Guibert discovered he was HIV-positive. Before this text, he was
not ill. Now, he is. This is the text both before and after "sida."

*Vous m'avez fait former des fantômes* is composed of three
parts. The longest, "Beaucoup de jeux de nuit" (lots of night
games) describes a group of kidnappers of children preparing
their victims for combat with infanteros. One child, 2, who regularly receives fellatio through the sack in which he is suspended—the mode of imprisonment for all the kidnapped
children—escapes. He is replaced with twins, but one dies in
combat. Pirate, one of the kidnappers, finds the corpse and rapes
it. Before being executed for allowing the death, Pirate utters
Sade's phrase: "vous m'avez fait former des fantômes." In the
second section, the group moves from the cave to the infanteros
practice field and the arena. This section relates preparations for
combat and several scenarios of battle. The third, very brief epi-
sode describes the end of the games, the public spectacles in the
arena as well as the erotic games in the cave. The games end with
the end of the novel.

Owen Heathcote compares Guibert's characters to Sade's
phantoms in this text because "different from Sade, whose phan-

toms represented a legitimate, compensatory and above all
imaginary outlet, the violently erotic phantoms of Pirate and
Lune have been rendered concrete."[22] Guibert's characters speak
Sade's phrase but render it literal. The key factor is in understanding the referent of the pronoun in the title: Who is the
"you" in the title of the text? It is the reader, but also the text
itself. Guibert "in the same way as the brigands, has it in for people like him, for his brother; he has it in for pleasure, at once ac-
complice and traitor of his own writing."[23] Both accusation and
inclusive seduction, the pronoun "vous," both formal and plural
"you," lures the reader into the text but chastises us for being
voyeurs. The reader creates phantoms; the writer exposes them
and reflects them back to us, ghosts in our own mirrors.

Bands of children stolen from their parents are trained to fight.
In fact, combats are arranged with allusions to Christian martyr-
dom (there is a subtextual reference to the Virgin, both the Christian icon and pre-sexual victim, an obvious allusion to the
sacrificial children). At the end, Aztec ritual killings continue to
lend religious overtones to the violence. Sexual violence is ritualized as it was in Sade. At the end, police want to disband the
group. Heathcote again compares this with Sade, for "adding on
Sade's text, Guibert suggests that phantoms of erotic violence
take pleasure in a generality and popularity that goes very far beyond the walls of any Silling castle."[24] The real motor of the sexual violence is profit when spectators come to view the children
fight in the arena. We all participate in this fight to the death. We
are guilty of blood lust and sexual lust. We are spectators to the
massacre as we are voyeurs in the text. We ourselves create the
phantoms of our own disgrace. Even Sade's ritual of depravity
would have been impossible without the four friends' fabulous
wealth. Readers and writers are caught in the sexual economy of
the text.

*Vouz m'avez fait former des fantômes* emphasizes castration,
the sexual body in pieces: The children are held in sacks and cas-
trated if need be. With the threat of sexual violence and imprisonment comes the inevitability of the body's dismemberment.
Fragmentation and the male body are linked in Guibert, more so
than in Sade. For the marquis, the mutilated body belonged
mostly, but not exclusively, to female victims; for Guibert, "by including a series of twin doubles and fragmented members on the

textual and on the sexual level, *Vous m'avez fait former des fantômes* proposes and parodies a sort of model, a pattern of the masculine body, a sort of testicular, phallic and seminal vision of literature."[25] Heathcote notes that, in *Vous m'avez fait former des fantômes,* the phantoms are "image-fantômes" as Guibert described them, which is images likened to death. *Vous m'avez fait former des fantômes* would therefore be "a stripping naked of eroticization and of the cruelty of death."[26] He notes that "while Sade's texts do not announce an escape, nor an alternative, nor retribution, Guibert's novel exposes, all the while playfully, its own delirium."[27] Unlike Sade, who tried to create his identity by choosing to turn his sexual fantasies into writing, Guibert does not want to create a rational framework of his text and of his sexuality, a system that can be decoded according to rational guidelines. Unlike Sade, he does not wish to accuse others of being guilty for making his phantoms. They are part of the way he approaches his sense of self. In this text, sex and violence are so intertwined it is difficult to tell if Guibert renders the violence banal, wishes to diminish its importance, or if he wishes to expose the game. One wonders in this game if, for Guibert, violence is inbred, if it comes from the culturally mandated rituals of the kidnappers and the infanteros. In the end, perhaps, it is the spectators who pay to see the show, in an economy of consumption reminiscent of Sade, who control whether or not the phantoms will reveal themselves. What remains of the body are the phantoms of extreme violence or sexuality that linger in the mind of those who bore witness to the spectacle, who relived the unspeakable acts in the texts.

As we have seen, photos too allow bodies to fragment and record their disarticulation on film. Saint-Amand says that in Guibert, photos always search not only for light but also for desire. The photo is always on stage, in an articulation of a system of phantoms.[28] Edna McCaffrey talks about the supernatural aspect of the photos, "several Guibertian photos . . . function through the invocation of a surreal world, even a supernatural one, by the angle of the objects that, according to their representation in the photographic space, evoke a preoccupation with the capacity for things to transform reality."[29]

In fact, Allen Grove reminds us of photography's phantom beginnings, especially with regard to the development of X-rays in

1895. He describes the first photographs as images that in some
ways contained ghostly remnants. Given the lengthy exposure
time of these early works, street scene photographs, for example,
sometimes included shadowy figures that passed before the camera during the eight-hour exposure.[30] To early observers, these
images may have seemed like essences of supernatural beings,
ghosts perhaps. So, too, Grove recalls, did the X-ray at first appear like a technology capable of capturing the invisible, to see
through flesh.[31] Grove declares, "The strange penetrative nature
of X-rays raised far more questions than it answered. The
Crookes Tube and the photographic plate mysteriously opened a
door into a world never before seen."[32] Guibert recaptures the
illusive quality of these first photographs by reinventing photographic ghosts.

Guibert's film *La Pudeur ou l'impudeur* provides a visual trace
of his refusal to disappear. The ghost image, at least, will remain
behind. Guibert was contacted by TF1 in summer 1990 to make
a film of his life in which he would be both subject and author.
The film was finished in March 1991. Chambers discusses *La Pudeur ou l'impudeur* as a phantom image because, "This narrative
of confrontation, transfer, and survival thus reveals itself to be
an allegorical reflection on the conditions and consequences of
representation, understood as a mode of *deliverance* for beings
subject to death but conditioned on a rule of communicability."[33]
This film allows its creator, already himself a phantom coming to
terms with his death, to be delivered by preserving himself on
film. In a way it restores a "reality" to the fiction where art takes
the place of the body. In fact, Buot rightly notes, this project
came at a time when reality shows were becoming huge hits in
France and they began to replace documentaries. "It's shock
television, with a brutal reality and the spectator transformed
into voyeur."[34] Guibert's project provides the ultimate "reality
TV" experience, where the television image completely replaces
the body already dead. Catherine Mavrikakis notes the elusive
nature of the video and its relation to the invisible when she
states video allows us to see what is present in the text; it has the
phantasmagoric nature of breath, of the invisible. The videogra-
pher's work is a phantom both Other and present. This absent
presence exists not only in Guibert's video work but in his writings as well. "It is also a case of seeing in Guibert, in parallel to

this breathless time, a slow time, a slow motion time of daily existence, a time outside of time it seems to me written more in
Guibert's cinema work or in his photographs: the time of the
fixed image. It is the encounter of two timeframes, each inscribed
apparently more into one medium than the other, in writing or
in the video, which will be staged here."[35]

For Guibert, phantoms of other texts and people, sexual incognito, point to the shadow that waits behind the text itself: death.
In his texts, there are suggestions of friends and acquaintances
dying of mysterious illnesses that in later texts is identified as
AIDS. Death lies in wait at the periphery of a life exploring sexuality. Subsequently, AIDS moves to the forefront of textuality in
later works as Guibert writes about his own body's life with AIDS
and the search for a cure. To some extent, sexuality is supplanted
by death as the nexus of the act of writing. Death is now the text.
In Sade and Guibert, the image of death shadows the act of writing. In many ways, the moment of death is also the moment of
the photograph. In fact, in this way, the realism of the camera eye
is called into question.

Phantom images appear in early text, as Worton recalls, such
as *My Parents.* Guibert takes a photo of his mother, for which she
has spent quite a while getting ready. Yet the camera does not
work properly and the image is lost. In other instances, Guibert
photographed his aged aunts in provocative poses as a way to
preserve them as they never were. In all the cases, as also in
*Ghost Image,* a text of photographs composed entirely of words,
Guibert tells us phantom images are not visual, they are simula-
cra of words. For Worton, "If the perfect image of his mother at
the height of her beauty, the one of the naked body of his aunt
Suzanne, or that of the happiness of the world are always to be
read and never to be seen, it is because the phantom image tends
to move towards something other that the image; it reaches
towards the narrative."[36] Perhaps there can be no perfect image
because the image always escapes. Only traces of it can remain,
the phantom images of the negative. Instead, writing may remain
as a lasting witness to the search for the ideal. As Sarkonak says,
we can speak of a "corporalité textuelle" when discussing the
materiality of Guibert's works. Leaving a physical trace behind by
writing as much as possible became an obsession.[37] The image

must give way to the materiality of the text, the only possible substitute for the body.

In *Ghost Image,* the text is divided into small segments, each
describing a type of photograph. The photographic image is already a ghost precisely because there are no photos here. The
text describes images, but there are no images with which to understand the text. Barthes says in *Camera Lucida* that photography represents an instant of reality that must have been at one
time but that is no longer. The image preserved represents by its
very nature always an absence. This trace of what was is akin to
desire, that after which we constantly yearn. It also represents
death because it always shows us what is no more. Desire and
death are always linked in photographs, always there in Guibert's
text. Traces remain, ghosts of what was.

Time cannot stop for the photo, the instant that was there. The
photo is witness to a reality that is always in the past, which can
never be exactly as it was again. Time—marking it, passing it,
holding on to it—is increasingly obsessive for Guibert. Mavrikakis looks at the speed with which Guibert condenses time, for
at the end of his life being young means being old. She equates
this with pornography: The text wants the reader to take pleasure
through asphyxiation, so the phrase strangles him or her.[38] In this
way, desire, time, and images converge, leaving only the traces of
the pencil jealously guarded from the hospital bed that will write
until the end.

Stéphane Grisi's analysis of autopathographies looks at Guibert's AIDS texts and says, "In the narration, Guibert privileges a
clinical narration of sickness. His texts are constituted by repeti-
tion and accumulation of subjective details on the multiplicity of
his symptoms, of exams that he undergoes and of his treatments."[39] This multiplication of details to expand our visual understanding of the texts hides a lack, however. Describing the
objects that make up a life cannot substitute for an integral body.
Behind these things lies a blank page. At the end, in this race
toward death, the details of the text can only help him recreate
an image of what was. As was the case in *Ghost Image,* words can
bring back to life the image of what is gone. We can say, along
with Emily Apter, that Guibert's novels are neither fiction nor
pure autobiography, and they somehow resemble notebooks
from the land of ghosts.[40]

Sade reveled in fragmenting the bodies of his characters, leaving body parts on the floor, witness to the ultimate sexual gratification. Bodies are consumed and discarded in a kind of economy of pleasure. Guibert too shows us images of bodies that are in pieces, at times with the pieces lined up on tables as was the case with several of his photographs. Here we have perhaps a consumerized vision, an excess of parts that renders the body inanimate. This bloody, physical, violent use of the body stems perhaps in both authors precisely from the fact that fragmentation may be the only possible outcome of the exploration to "say everything" about the self, about identity, about sexuality, about the body. When nothing is off limits, the body has reached the limit of its usefulness.

When the body disappears, a trace remains. Sade and Guibert hope it will be present in their writing. Guibert explicitly says in later texts such as *Cytomegalovirus* that writing is a substitute for the disappearing body. Sade, too, in a more violent way, shows though his excessive need to write seemingly endlessly that writing must be the freedom his body no longer has. This trace, this phantom is his "realized phantom," the new language that Sade alluded to in his letters. The phantoms of sexual conquests, the need for those images to become real, become in Sade a mechanism for survival.

If we take the totality of Guibert's work—writing, photography, and video—we see that fragmentation was always in many ways a theme. The loneliness of body parts dissociated from bodies becomes a metaphor for the solitude of the act of writing. Despite moments of bravado, of explicit shock value, Guibert's narrators are often on the outside looking in, waiting for treatments, alone on islands, neglected by parents. The gradual disappearance of the body becomes the central metaphor of Guibert's work as he prepares to leave only his writing behind.

# 6

## Bodies in/as Evidence: Conclusion

Bodies leave evidence of their existence at first, but this physical trace disintegrates with time. The text itself, perhaps, is the ghost that remains behind. Bodies perform sexual acts before our eyes in Sade and Guibert, but those bodies already begin to lose hold of a firm sense of identity. They shift identity, assume multiple masks, get lost in time, are imprisoned, and ultimately disappear through violence, disease, or neglect. The body of work left behind is the only evidence of existence.

In the preceding chapters, we explored the ways in which the Marquis de Sade influenced Hervé Guibert. We saw that the contemporary French writer acknowledged his debt to the libertine, among others, in his literary sensibility. We also saw that Sade's influence among post-World War II intellectuals is undeniable. Still, critical voices rise up for and against Sade, whose reputation still arouses passions. Certainly, however, the preceding discussion has included very contradictory assessments of Sade's works in authors who often decry him as a lightweight or champion him as a thinker. In what ways was Sade merely a writer of his age? Francine du Plessix Gray notes Donatien was vulnerable to more severe punishment than his peers because of his family history, including a father who had already caused scandal. Also, he was a lonely man, socially isolated, refusing to visit the king's court.[1]

She also notes:

A pariah even within his own caste, Sade would for decades after his death be simultaneously stigmatized by the excesses of the monarchy and of the Terror. The coalition of bourgeois capitalists and repatriated émigrés who took power under the Bourbon Restoration saw him as an emblem of the bloodshed unleashed in 1789, as "one of the most odious fruits of the crisis." Good republicans such as Michelet, the theorist of revolutionary fraternity and idolizer of "The

126

People," demonized him as a symbol of ancien régime corruption: "That such a man still lived—there was no better proof of the need to destroy the hideous arbitrariness of the old monarchy," Michelet wrote in 1848. "He was a professor emeritus of crime. Societies end with such monstrous events: the Middle Ages with Gilles de Retz [Rais], the famous killer of children; the ancien régime with Sade, apostle of assassins."[2]

Gray sees Sade as a writer whom subsequent intellectuals were glad to vilify. We have also seen that, to some extent, it is accepted that the authorities made Sade a scapegoat for his class. "Tired of seeing noble offenders get away with their crimes, the public wanted an example to be set, and the marquis de Sade proved a convenient scapegoat" after the Arcueil affair, according to Lever.[3] Sade made a good target because he never denied his predilections, and there was enmity between the marquis's father and the court of Louis XV.

Sade as writer seems difficult for many critics. His reputation as a libertine is, however, not controversial, unlike his reputation as a man of letters. In an age that in some ways is considered the apogee of French thought, philosophical above all, with writers such as Voltaire, Rousseau, Diderot, Beaumarchais, and on and on, rehabilitating Sade as a philosopher occupies much critical debate. Louisa Shea in fact explains that Sade was one of the most noted cynics, in the ancient tradition, but he transformed cynicism from an act of public frankness into an act of hypocrisy. Sade transferred cynic indecency by sexualizing it, "but he nevertheless remained true to Cynic shamelessness insofar as his depictions of sexual acts are deliberately provocative, intended to unseat our sense of what is right, proper or natural."[4] In this he was heir to his Enlightenment colleagues who undermined authority by questioning codes of behavior.

Although he condemns him as an unoriginal thinker, Bongie does acknowledge "a more likely development in Sade's future literary fortunes might involve increased recognition that it is really the marquis' correspondence—most notably his prison letters—that deserves to be honored as great literature and accorded some measure of the praise that has been lavished almost superstitiously on his novels."[5] For Bongie, these impassioned letters constantly invent the man. They are filled with lies both to himself and to others, poured out in molten rhetoric, humorous at times if nearly always tinged with prison paranoia. But despite his criticism of Sade's letters, Bongie says they will no doubt remain his most lasting literary achievement, his true masterpiece.

In terms of his fictional writing, Bongie sees that Sade's novels conform to the tradition of eighteenth-century philosophical novels that become vehicles for the author's pet ideas. In his novels, he expounds on determinism, materialism, egotism, atheism, the evils of religion and jurisprudence, and the absurdity of remorse. "It is nearly impossible to distinguish the nuances separating the rhetoric of his personal correspondence from the parallel 'monster-speak' of his novels."[6] Bongie's statement here suggests that, for Sade, literary production and life experiences converge as the fictional works produced in prison and the letters sent from prison dovetail in tone and style. Writing of all kinds becomes an escape from confinement.

Bongie concludes quite unfavorably on Sade's characters when he notes, "In their actions, the monsters of the Sadean novels exemplify a complete fusion, a total integration of the marquis' conceiving and doing equation. They *do* whatever can be *conceived.* For them the only crime lies in exercising restraint, in not carrying their excesses through to the ultimate limit. In real life, Sade could experiment with only the limited interplay of imagining and acting out, at times allowing himself, nevertheless, a significant degree of 'overlap.'"[7]

Interestingly enough, although clearly Bongie considers Sade unfavorably when compared to his peers, he notes the extreme nature of Sade's characters. They exemplify the idea we have highlighted as crucially at the crossroads between Sade and Guibert: the necessity of doing whatever can be conceived, of totality. Also crucial for Sade is the interplay between imagining and acting out. The phantoms must be realized.

Other critics have been more enthusiastic about Sade as a writer perhaps, as we have said previously, because tackling the works of this philosophical iconoclast means redefining one's own philosophical positions with respect to the status quo. For many earlier critics of Sade, it became important to establish Sade's place in eighteenth-century philosophy and letters. For Blanchot, "In seeing similar formulations one after another, we begin to think that there is a discrepancy in Sade's thought, something missing, a madness. We sense a profoundly deranged thought, bizarrely suspended over the void. But, suddenly, logic assumes control, our objections vanish, and the system gradually takes shape."[8] He continues, "If crime is the spirit of Nature, there can be no crime against nature, and consequently no crime is possible. Sade asserts this, sometimes with great satisfaction, sometimes fiery rage."[9] Blanchot understands Sade's initial seeming incongruity as a partial return to the order and control championed by many writers and thinkers of his age, where systemic processes dominate. Still, an energy in Sade goes beyond the bounds of total control, and that makes his work somewhat unique.

Sade also reminds us of the tendencies of eighteenth-century writers to use rationalism to explore the limits of religions. Pierre Klossowski states, "Atheism, the supreme act of normative reason, is thus destined to establish the reign of the total absence of norms."[10] For Sade, atheism, reason, and rationality actually suggest absence, the void of reason.

So we could sum up some of these wide-ranging views as does Dalia Judovitz. "Through his exhaustive exposition of sexuality Sade succeeds in expanding its meaning, not only to include perverse and even criminal modes of activity, but also to challenge all moral referents, and thus fundamentally to alter the very definition of the limits of thought."[11] Clearly, although a definitive conclusion to the legacy of the Marquis de Sade proves difficult given the violently opposed opinions about his work, either as revolutionary thinker or literary fraud, Sade's influence reveals itself more nuanced than expected. Sade does change the face of eighteenth-century letters; he adds a new dimension to the Age of Reason. His texts, although censured and often published either anonymously or under pseudonyms to protect the author, benefited from a wide circulation. Undeniably, then, although relegated to the hell of the Bibliothèque Nationale for many decades following his death, during his lifetime, Sade's works carried weight. That is why we can see how his texts fit into the larger panorama of eighteenth-century literature to begin uncovering his legacy.

In many eighteenth-century works of literature, despite a general intellectual desire to reveal all through taxonomic classifications, picaresque ramblings, or philosophical musings on

quasiheretical subjects, texts from this period tend to elide discussions of physical sexuality. There existed a sort of litotic discussion of physical love. This is not to say that discussions of love
were absent, quite the contrary. But, aside from other libertine
texts from the seventeenth and eighteenth centuries, love was
chaste for the most part. Texts such as those of Marivaux, for example, abound with discussion of sentiment and emotion. In
Rousseau's *La Nouvelle Héloïse* (*The New Heloise*), Goethe's *The
Sorrows of Young Werther,* and Ugo Foscolo's *Le Ultime lettere di
Jacopo Ortis* (*The Last Letters of Jacopo Ortis*)—texts of the budding Romantic period—Sade's works stand out in contrast for
their frank discussion of sexual encounters. In this, he belongs
more to an earlier period, when comic libertine novels discussed
sexual escapades in hilarious detail. Although eighteenth-century
texts explore inanimate bodies and discuss them as machines or
as anatomical constructions, Sade explores sexuality. He is even
considered one of the first writers to understand female sexuality
by locating female pleasure in the clitoris. Sade's Juliette is the
libertine whore par excellence, as Norberg understands her: an
independent, sensual, sensible, and skilled practitioner with a
healthy sexual appetite for varied sexual practices.[12] Moreover,
Sade's writing, while clearly misogynistic on many levels, does
also discuss female sexuality and pleasure. In this, he was radical
for his time. Although often traced to Pietro Aretino's text *Ragio-
namenti* from 1534, pornography as we know it is a fairly recent
phenomenon. In the seventeenth and eighteenth centuries, pornography was mainly French, and it has been a primarily Western
concept.[13] During Sade's era, pornography was largely political,
with Queen Marie Antoinette a prime butt of the jokes, reflecting
an underlying anxiety about the role of women and the mainte-
nance of gender boundaries.[14] For Lynn Hunt, Sade's novels
marked an important transition in that he took the subversive
possibilities of pornography to their extreme and thus forced the
way to apolitical pornography. After Sade, pornography was
identified with a general assault on morality rather than specific
criticism of the political system.[15]

So really, his texts provide a counterweight to the "scientific,"
descriptive, empirical way of looking at organisms and at organic
systems. He provides fodder for his enemies, but that certainly
was his intention. He turns the newly nascent interest in rational,

dispassionate observation on its head. By bringing discussion of sexuality into the center of his works, and then bringing these discussions to extreme limits, Sade also pushes Enlightenment thinking to the edge.

In this, Sade provides a precursor for Guibert. Whatever Sade's influence on the world of letters—and that is clearly still debated—he did provide a model for some of Guibert's thinking about bodies. Guibert, too, allows himself to exist on the margins by provoking his readers to extremes. He proposes bodies for our viewing in a way that seems like we are at a peep show or intruding on an autopsy. In *Les Chiens*, the narrator—and by extension the reader—literally registers the lovemaking of the couple he will join by listening in on them, aurally peeping through the floor. Just as Sade constructed a literary discourse at odds with his own century, so too did Guibert take the twentieth century's highly anesthetized medical discourse and apply it to the most wrenching descriptions of his own dying body. We know we are watching a human being die, and in this age of tell-all media but insularity from death, Guibert provokes his readers into discomfort. Both Sade and Guibert accomplish their desire to intimidate though language, through texts, and through the act of storytelling.

Like Sade's works, Guibert's also reflect their historical moment: the AIDS years. Genon notes the paucity of work on Guibert, especially in French universities. Few dissertations and scholarly texts have appeared before 2004, Genon says. Why this reticence to discuss Guibert? For Genon, it may have to do with "a general mistrust of homosexuality, more specifically of homosexual literature in France."[16] Guibert, then, reshapes our understanding of identity. In his analysis of Guibert as gay writer, Lawrence Schehr says that Guibert takes the basic formula of "normative representation, that of identity and of opposition, and deconstructs it to annihilate the idea of opposition without there being consequences for this action."[17] This would explain a text like *Les Chiens* and why it begins with a scene of voyeurism of a man watching a heterosexual couple.

In Guibert, bodies provide evidence of foiled cures, of loves lost, and of lives lived. His entire corpus is about the corps: bodies in love, bodies dying, bodies exploring their limits. Bodies are a centering theme, as they were for Sade. Taking control of the

body and keeping control of the decaying corpse become metaphors for creativity. The body is the work, and working on bodies
to dismember them, to love them, to possess them, and to keep
them alive become moments that give rhythm to their work. For
Derek Duncan, "The virtual omnipresence of Guibert's body in
the image invites the spectator to consider the body as a text that
works as a signature, as a metonymy of the self."[18]

To reconstitute the body, Guibert must go public, bring it on
stage. For Worton, Guibert's "famous unveiling of self is nothing
but a pretext to constantly stage or restage the subject on trial: by
dramatizing and 'theatricalizing' his self and his body (often with
real or metaphorical mirrors) he connotes an identity to be realized instead of denoting a fixed, findable identity."[19] Guibert's
need to "write until the end" produces narrative subversion. Tra-
ditional genres do not work as vehicles for expressions of the
Other—a gay man, a man with AIDS. Subversive writing provides
the only narrative possibility.

In the face of illness and death, intimacy becomes untenable.
The body becomes public as it is unveiled before doctors, as
friends must confess to lovers they may have infected, as writers
reveal their struggles with varying stages of bodily decay.

Are Guibert's texts as transgressive as those of Sade? Worton
says, "In a sense Guibert's sexographic texts conform to the rules
of pornography that demand the absence of facial descriptions,
the schematization of characters and the lack of narrative logic.
Just as the pornographer, Guibert as transgressive writer forces
readers to revert to their own experiences to fill the gaps and thus
makes them not only collaborators or co-creators but also ac-
complices."[20]

In the end, perhaps, Worton says it best when he redefines
Guibert's texts not as pornography but as erotic works. "The big
secret of his whole work, always repeated, is that all genres are
suspect and that it is only by erasing all generic distinction that
one can construct a satisfying eroticism and an ontology of the
authentic being."[21]

In some ways, Guibert and Sade are profoundly egotistical.
Self-preservation and asserting identity become primary impulses for both. For Sade, preservation may be necessary in an
era of political instability, where the body politic was subsuming
individuality. The dying regime during the last vestiges of its

power and the torturers in Sade's text manifest this impulse on individual victims. For Guibert, egotism may be self-preservation. Clinging to vestiges of personal power afforded through the act of writing reconfirms the self, allowing the body one more day before the end.

In a very modern literary gesture, in *The 120 Days of Sodom,* the narrator often addresses the reader. At the beginning of the text, as the characters' journey toward Silling begins, the narrator challenges our prurience as we contemplate what is to come. "If we had not said everything, analyzed everything, how could you expect us to guess what suited you?"[22] That is the essence of Sade's literary project: saying everything, revealing everything. As readers, he tells us he knows we are searching for something he can give us, and had he not said everything, we would perhaps be left unsatisfied. So we are in fact creating this text along with the marquis, challenging him to provoke us with sexuality that moves inexorably toward death, and then we must remain to count the bodies at the end, to tally them up on the ledger sheet. Sade's extreme gesture and his extravagant texts are merely what we want without knowing it. Seeking to know all, even that which will destroy us, is after all the impulse itself to be enlightened.

For Guibert, *Le Mausolée des amants* represents a final possibility for saying it all, revealing his "real" journal and truly writing to the end as he had hoped. In it, he mentions many artists and musicians whose work influences him: Whitman, Van Gogh, Zola, Melville, Bach, and Proust, to name a very few from a long list. Some authors are mentioned several times: Peter Handke, Dostoyevsky, and Kafka especially. He also mentions several films, Hollywood classics and French films. In this journal, as we have seen, Guibert mentions that he read Lely's biography of Sade. Only a few entries previous to this citation he shows interest in possibly working on a text that involves toreros (a theme in *Vous m'avez fait former des fantômes*). Shortly after mentioning his discovery of Lely's text, Guibert begins to work on it:

A movement like a whirlwind that pulls me to the end (of the second part) of *Fantômes:* finishing or just getting by? Who is making me finish in one day what I would usually have taken two or three days to finish, and which as a result leaves me sad and numb? I'm overcome

in reading the first part, which seems rather bad to me, confused: de-
pornography all this? Clean up each sentence? I think again about
Handke, who has such confidence in the diary—doesn't the novel always carry within it its own erasure?[23]

Guibert struggles to finish this most Sadean text; he's already
working on his next text, just as this text began germinating in his
mind as he worked on *My Parents*. He later mentions that he also
struggles with the corrections to the text once it has been accepted for publication. *Vous m'avez fait former des fantômes* represents for him all writing, all fiction, in that it carries within itself
perhaps the power of its own destruction, of its own erasure.

Reading Sade becomes clearly an impetus toward writing, a
process that becomes painful but necessary. He struggles with
this text even after its completion. Guibert is in some way allowing the marquis's phrases to shape his work: the text is a phantom that *must* come to life. There is an urgency in his work here,
as Sade's phrase itself suggests ("il faut," I must make these
phantoms real) that will continue to propel Guibert forward until
he dies, unable to type the last pages of his journal for publication. The phantom has indeed come to life, the ghostly white
pages left behind as only witnesses.

Revealing all, saying it all. By not hiding anything, the body becomes the reader's obsession as well. These bodies described,
laid bare, and tortured are also our own. We see ourselves in
Guibert's texts through the eyes of the doctor whose gaze reveals
little. Sex itself becomes anguish when torturers must find victims to continue their destruction. This anguish may also be our
own as we come to realize that writing, after all, is not enough.
There is a certain unfulfillment in the text that extinguishes itself.
It makes us ask if we can ever hope to really leave a trace. We
delude ourselves that our children will bear witness to us and
that our good works and those who knew us will speak for us;
what we made will remain. Guibert makes us question our desires as human beings to leave something behind. Perhaps it is
all illusion; when our identity goes, we go with it. As we live the
moment of writing as the text evolves before our eyes, we know
we will run out of text, just as the author ran out of time.

# Notes

## INTRODUCTION

1. To date, the following texts have been translated: *To the Friend Who Did Not Save My Life, My Parents, Gangsters, Paradise, Cytomegalovirus, Ghost Images, Blindsight, The Compassion Protocol,* and *The Man in the Red Hat,* approximately a third of Guibert's literary production.

2. Notable among monographs and biographies on Guibert in French are those by Jean-Pierre Boulé and François Buot. Stéphane Grisi and Bruno Blanckeman dedicate chapters of their books in French to Guibert, as do David Caron and Ross Chambers, who both wrote about Guibert in English. Two collections of essays have appeared on Guibert: the Nottingham Studies from 1995 and the collection edited by Ralph Sarkonak in 1997, *Le corps textuel de Hervé Guibert.*

3. As James A. Steintrager explains, it may be no surprise that Sade was rediscovered in the 1960s. "At the time, Sade was enjoying considerable exposure and his name brought with it a certain bawdy cachet; while the Marquis was certainly not somehow constitutive of 1960s culture, he was a reference of some importance from high theory to pop culture and many stops in between" (Steintrager, "Liberating Sade," 352).

4. I will speak in following chapters of disarticulation and of disintegration. Disarticulation will refer both to fragmenting the body into component parts or being unable to articulate verbally what one sees and feels. In Guibert, disarticulation precedes disintegration, where the body vanishes.

5. As Ralph Sarkonak explains it in the introduction to a collection of essays on Guibert, "autofiction" consists of texts that straddle the artificial barrier critics like to erect between "fiction" and "non fiction," forgetting that all texts are a mise-en-scène of their own "truth" (Sarkonak, "Hervé Guibert: Vice des formes" 6).

6. Guibert certainly was familiar with the work of major French intellectuals of the 1950s, 1960s, and 1970s who wrote on Sade (such as De Beauvoir, Barthes, and Bataille) given his illustrious circle of intellectual friends and acquaintances, including Barthes, Michel Foucault et al.

7. Sade became a role model or case study for numerous authors, filmmakers, and artists. The surrealists hailed him as a precursor, alluding to his works in their art, writing, and films. Georges Bataille discusses Sade's language. Camus sees him as the ultimate rebel. Pasolini relates the decay of fascist ideology to the world Sade created in his film *Salo' or The 120 Days of Sodom.*

Of course, Sade also came to exemplify sexual pathologies still named for him. Just as Sade's writings reflect the dark underside of the Age of Enlightenment, so too were his descriptions of sexuality understood as emblematic of sexual deviance. Interest in Sade's works as proof of a psychological or behavioral phenomenon goes back to Richard von Kraff-Ebing (1840–1900), chair of psychology and neurology at the University of Vienna, who coined the term *masochism* after the writings of Sacher-Masoch. In contrast to Sacher-Masoch's visions of erotic pleasure derived from inflicting pain on oneself, Sade's experiments in sexuality often are reduced to vague ideas of cruelty toward another object outside the self. The names of both psychopathologies were united into the concept *sadomasochism,* a term relating to arousal through inflicting pain on oneself or on an object of desire other than the self.

Since then, revisions of Kraff-Ebing's work have provided nuanced analysis to further denote the difference between sadistic and masochistic deviances. When exploring the body's transgressions, Sigmund Freud's analyses of sexual deviance named for Sade provide classifications. More so than previous psychoanalysts, Jacques Lacan addresses Sade in his totality. Gilles Deleuze questions the entity known as sadomasochism. He maintains that Sade is better known than Masoch, and that the latter's work "has nothing to do with that of Sade. Their techniques differ, and their problems, their concerns and their intentions are entirely dissimilar" (Deleuze, *Masochism,* 13). In each of the studies cited, Sade's works have been considered testimonials for ways in which the body can be appropriated, manipulated, dominated, and destroyed. Sadism as understood in Kraff-Ebing and Freud involves inflicting pain on victims' bodies. Lacan moves from this position to one that bridges philosophy and psychoanalysis. Sade is a critical figure for Guibert also because of his importance for psychoanalytic writing on the body and sexuality.

8. Many critical essays on Sade refer to the marquis as a *philosophe,* a sort of negative image, in a moral sense, of his contemporaries. Here, however, I'm making a distinction to show how Sade inverted the discourse of his contemporaries. Whether or not Sade can be considered a *philosophe* is not entirely central to my purpose here.

9. Furthermore, many authors have been "read through" Sade: Adam Smith, Diderot, Voltaire, Robespierre, Freud, Lacan, Bataille, and De Beauvoir.

10. "Par exemple, vous avez imaginé faire merveille, je le parierais, en me réduisant à une abstinence atroce sur le *péché de la chair.* Eh bien, vous vous êtes trompés: vous m'avez fait former des fantômes qu'il faudra que je réalise" (Lely, *Sade,* Letter CLXII, 397).

In this study, I will quote English translations of French text throughout. Where published translations of secondary texts exist, I will quote only from the translations. Where primary text translations exist, or where I have translated primary or secondary texts myself, I will include the original quotation in endnotes. All published translations used are cited in the bibliography.

11. "Tu connais quand même tes livres, n'est-ce pas" (Guibert, *Protocole,* 132).

12. "Je ne vois pas de bonne oeuvre qui soit méchante. Le fameux principe de délicatesse de Sade. J'ai l'impression d'avoir fait une oeuvre barbare et délicate" (Guibert, *Protocole,* 132).

13. "Charmante créature, vous voulez mon linge sale, mon vieux linge? Savez-vous que c'est d'une délicatesse achevée? Vous voyez comme je sens le prix des choses. Écoutez, mon ange, j'ai toute l'envie du monde de vous satis-

faire sur cela, car vous savez que je respecte les goûts, les fantaisies: quelque baroques qu'elles soient, je les trouve toutes respectables, et parce qu'on n'en est pas le maître, et parce que la plus singulière et la plus bizarre de toutes, bien analysée, remonte toujours à un principe de délicatesse," Sade's letter of November 23–24, 1783, quoted in Barthes, *Sade, Fourier, Loyola* (French edition), 174.

14. "Je sens une impression de bonheur physiologique, de tranquillité, je sens mon corps plein de merde et je sais qu'il va pouvoir l'évacuer" (Guibert, *Mausolée*, 365).

15. "Sade dessine la topographie de rêve d'un établissement de luxure: les salles de fustigation et de torture s'ouvrent simplement sur un cimetière" (ibid.).

16. Buot, *Hervé Guibert*, 72.

17. Eribon, "Hervé Guibert," 88.

18. Barthes, *Sade*, 170–71. In the translation of Barthes's text, the French "délicatesse," becomes "tact," not "sensitivity" as it does in the translation of the letter provided earlier.

19. Michael Worton goes so far as to talk of treason. "Few writers since Genet have had a taste for treason as acute as Guibert. His parents, his aunts Louise and Suzanne, his friends (Foucault, Gina Lollobrigida, Isabelle Adjani, and many others less famous) are all betrayed by this writer who thinks it is his right to deliver their secrets" ("Peu d'écrivains depuis Genet ont eu autant que Guibert le goût de la trahison. Ses parents, ses tantes Louise et Suzanne, ses amis [Foucault, Gina Lollobrigida, Isabelle Adjani, et bien d'autres moins célèbres] sont tous trahis par cet écrivain qui s'arroge le droit de livrer 'leurs' secrets") (Worton, "En (d)écrivant," 71). Guibert's sense of self depends on unmasking the complicity of those to whom he is close.

20. "Serait inhérent à toute parole qui concerne de près la mort" (Décarie, "Protocole," 246).

21. Caron, *AIDS*, 141.

22. I emphasize the distinction here between identity, the condition of being oneself or itself, the sense of self, providing sameness and continuity in personality over time, and identification, an act or instance of identifying, the state of being identified, acceptance as one's own of the values and interest of a social group, a process by which one ascribes to oneself the qualities or characteristics of another person, perception of another as an extension of oneself (Webster's College Dictionary printed version 1995).

23. "Une sorte de mythologie, de vision épique du corps et des pulsions" (Bellour, "Guibert," 81).

24. Butler, *Bodies*, 2.

25. ibid.

26. In the present study, I rely on examples from several of Sade's novels, but most of the examples come from his first, darkest full text. *The 120 Days of Sodom* proves a valuable text for discussion because it brings together Sade's philosophy in a narrative space that is a theater of physical depravity. Of Guibert's texts studied in the following chapters, I concentrate on those that provide the richest material for the present discussion, but I consider most of his texts at least briefly.

27. "Il y a chez Hervé une jubilation liée au plaisir physique dont il parle vo-

lontiers et qu'il associe à la souffrance. La vision du monde sadienne, Hervé la connaît bien" (Buot, *Hervé Guibert*, 92).

## CHAPTER 1. IRRESISTIBLE BIOGRAPHIES

1. "Tout comme Montaigne (Guibert) est toujours le sujet de son oeuvre" (Boulé, *Voices*, 527).
2. "La libération de l'homosexualité—ou plus exactement de la bissexualité—constitue l'un des acquis les plus spectaculaires. Mais il n'aura profité qu'aux élites: le roi et sa Cour, les artistes en renom, quelques intellectuels" (Lever, *Bûchers*, 87).
3. Trumbach, "Erotic," 254.
4. Trumbach, *Sex*, 6.
5. Caron, *AIDS*, 23
6. In discussing the period in which Sade lived, Lever also notes a radical shift in thinking about the body and the homosexual body. Under Louis XIII, libertinage was not only a moral affair but also an issue of ideas. Libertine writers and thinkers brought issues of sexuality into the open, so they become fodder for intellectual debate, not merely exposition. The libertine of this period was not necessarily a bon vivant, but he did not submit unconditionally to the Church's dogma. He places reason and analysis at the center of ethics, and loudly demands independence of thought. To partially substantiate his claim to a greater openness toward homosexual behavior, Lever notes that a confrèrie of homosexuals existed during the eighteenth century right in Versailles' court (Lever, *Bûchers*, 156 and 200).
7. Rey, "Police,"129.
8. Ibid., 131.
9. Ibid., 143.
10. Van der Meer, "Persecutions," 266.
11. Lever, *Bûchers*, 397.
12. Hekma, "Sodomites," 433.
13. Ibid., 441.
14. Ibid., 442.
15. The political climate of the age certainly encouraged Sade's darker side as well. When Sade père came to Paris from his provincial home, he entered the center of the world of transgression. After an early libertine period, the final years of Louis XIV's long reign were more conservative. The reign of his successor Louis XV was known for its libertine tendencies. Although the king himself was considered a prude, he was said to revel in reading the vice squad's detailed police reports and had a homosexual affair at the age of fourteen. Censure was an effective weapon against transgression, but often only against the lower and middle class.

At times, the nobility created scandal for openly bisexual behavior, also called "le vivre italien." The vice police regularly patrolled the Tuileries gardens around the Louvre, the main thoroughfare for prostitutes at the time. Aristocrats were picked up on charges of soliciting and other crimes, but they were often released without sentencing. At most, they received a short, forty-eight-hour stay in the Bastille prison, but almost never in the Bicêtre or Châtelet prisons, both infamous because they housed common criminals. The Bastille was a prison for political prisoners, religious criminals, and prisoners of the press. There was only one sodomite there between 1690 and 1705. It was for prisoners that the government did not want to judge in public. The horrible Châtelet, on the other hand, held prisoners from modest means, but rarely bourgeois and nobles (Lever, *Bûchers*, 204). Bicêtre was a dank place that no one spoke of, a hospice, an insane asylum, and a house of arrest (ibid., 207).

Donatien's father in fact was incarcerated for a few days when caught soliciting a young male informant posing as a prostitute. He later established a liaison with the king's young new wife and, in order to be closer to her without attracting suspicion, married her maid-in-waiting, Marie Eléonore de Maillé de Carman.

16. The first recorded incident that many biographers believe showed the budding marquis's penchant for cruelty is when, at the age of four, he beat his playmate Louis Joseph de Bourbon, Prince de Condé, in front of ladies at the court. Following this incident, he was shipped back to Saumur in Provence to the care of his uncle, the Abbé. A noted libertine, the Abbé introduced his nephew to deviant sexual behavior in the relative seclusion of the Abbey. At the age of ten, Donatien returned to Paris to be educated by the Jesuits at the prestigious Collège Louis-le-Grand.

17. This affair brought into play Sade's mother-in-law, by most accounts the main negative force in Sade's life. Sade had shown signs of being a difficult character before she married her daughter to him. Still, marrying into such an old house was irresistible for the Présidente de Montreuil. As Sade's escapades continued, she tried to suppress them. In fact, la Présidente bought Keller off so that she would not press charges, but the media attention to the affair had made Sade's complete acquittal impossible. Sade's mother-in-law tried to mitigate the damage caused by her son-in-law, hoping he would eventually settle down. However, once Sade began an affair with his sister-in-law Anne Prospère, in 1772, his mother-in-law turned against him definitively. She began to cooperate with authorities to capture Sade.

By this point, Sade had established a reputation as one of the most extreme libertines. This inevitably led to royal disfavor. At the birth of his first son in 1767, the prince and princess of Condé acquiesced to being godparents, an honor reserved for only the most established and respected nobility. At the birth of his second son two years later, the royal couple did not participate. After the Keller affair, Sade escaped to the south of France and for some time, things calmed down.

18. Dried Spanish fly, sometimes called "blisterbug," at times taken internally as a diuretic, also considered an aphrodisiac, was derived from the cantharis beetle. This potion can be toxic if taken in large doses (*Dorland's Medical Dictionary*).

19. He also once wrote a letter in his own blood to his mother-in-law.

20. Lever describes in detail the types of letters used to incarcerate political prisoners in Sade's time. The *lettre de cachet* was a normal letter, folded over, with the name and address of the addressee, but with a band of paper around it carrying the royal seal in red wax. This was sent out only on the pleasure of the prince. Sade was a victim of this type of arbitrary accusation several times (Lever, *Bûchers*, 201).

21. "Joue sans cesse sur ce double statut d'aristocrate et de penseur, de seigneur imbu de ses droits héréditaires et de philosophe revendiquant une liberté nouvelle" (Delon, *Sade*, xvii). "Sade est ainsi devenu un personnage de légende, un être romanesque dont la destinée, de génération en génération, attire la greffe d'épisodes nouveaux . . . Sade assume dans son écriture tous les contes dont il a fait l'objet. Il redouble l'emprisonnement subi par un emprisonnement volontaire dans le ressassement des fantasmes sociaux confondus avec les siens propres. Il fait miroiter dans ses romans les images que l'opinion publique lui a renvoyées de lui-même" (ibid., xx).

22. Ibid., xxiv.

23. "L'écriture sadienne se nourrit d'un battement entre le raisonnement articulé et l'exacerbation du fantasme, entre le blasphème et l'euphémisme, la crudité et l'allusion" (ibid., lii). "L'oeuvre est ainsi tendue par une dynamique qui est celle de la progression de l'écriture et de la lecture, en même temps que celle d'un désir qui ne peut se rassasier d'une quelconque réalisation" (ibid., lii).

24. "Si le sadisme, selon sa formule, n'est que 'le contenu grossier (vulgaire) du texte sadien,' l'essentiel, d'un point de vue à la fois raffiné et élitiste, est dans la grammaire qui organise les postures, les épisodes, les scènes, et dans l'invention de la langue, capable de les dire" (ibid., xlvii). "Comme les romans épistolaires contemporains, la composition de Sade entraîne une complicité du lecteur, changé en voyeur" (ibid., lii). "L'Encyclopédie prétendait offrir le monde à voir et à comprendre sous forme d'un tableau. Encyclopédiste du mal, Sade suggère les limites d'une telle visibilité. Le désir, pour se perpétuer, doit réinventer des cabinets secrets et des manies inimaginables" (ibid., lvi).

25. "Hercule, vraiment taillé comme le dieu dont on lui donna le nom" (Sade, *Oeuvres*, Vol. 1, 50).

26. "Antinoüs, ainsi nommé parce qu'à l'exemple du bardache d'Hadrien, il joignait au plus beau vit du monde le cul le plus voluptueux" (Sade, *Oeuvres*, Vol. 1, 50–51).

27. "Brise-cul avait un hochet si plaisamment contourné qu'il lui devenait presque impossible d'enculer sans briser le cul" (Sade, *Oeuvres*, Vol. 1, 51).

28. "Bande-au-ciel, ainsi nommé parce que son érection, quelque chose qu'il fît, était perpétuelle," (Sade, *Oeuvres*, Vol. 1, 51).

29. "Vous voilà hors de France, au fond d'une forêt inhabitable, au-delà de montagnes escarpées dont les passages ont été rompus aussitôt après que vous les avez eu franchis. Vous êtes enfermées dans une citadelle impénétrable; qui que ce soit ne vous y sait; vous êtes soustraites à vos amis, à vos parents, vous êtes déjà mortes au monde, et ce n'est plus que pour nos plaisirs que vous respirez" (Sade, *Oeuvres*, Vol. 1, 66).

30. "Songez que ce n'est point du tout comme des créatures humaines que nous vous regardons, mais uniquement comme des animaux que l'on nourrit pour le service qu'on en espère et qu'on écrase de coups quand ils se refusent à ce service" (Sade, *Oeuvres*, Vol. 1, 68).

31. Dall'Orto, "Nature," 95–96.

32. Guibert's film *La Pudeur ou l'impudeur* was to be shown on TF1 on January 19, 1992, a few weeks after Guibert's death. The show was pulled at the last minute but subsequently shown at a late hour on January 30. Although some contradictions of the sequence of events emerged, by most accounts, the ethics

committee of the station received a letter from Solidarité Plus, a group working for HIV-positive individuals. Some reports of the event say they were against a "coup médiatique" of this kind. Then, another letter came, this time from the Conseil Supérieur de l'Audiovisuel, saying the National AIDS Council wanted to see the film before it was shown on TV. There was some confusion as to what really happened, because representatives of the two organizations later denied many parts of the official accounts of why the film was hidden from the larger viewing audience.

33. Arnaud Genon reminds us that these twenty-eight works include novels, novellas, short stories, essays, a photo collection, a script, his journal published posthumously, and a film.

34. Blanckeman identifies three cycles of Guibert's novels: young age, adult age, sick age. The first cycle describes a young deranged man. The second cycle is fragmented because the author cannot dissociate life from writing. In the third cycle, death gives structure to the works (Blanckeman, *Récits*, 92).

35. Caron, *AIDS*, 117.

36. *Vice* is a photo novel where Guibert explores hidden deserted zones in Paris such as museum basements after hours and taxidermy shops. He reprises the role of flâneur first popularized by Charles Baudelaire and later by the surrealists Louis Aragon and André Breton, along with Apollinaire, their early twentieth century contemporary. But Guibert turns his steps to the catacombs, not the boulevards of the capital. On his promenade, he describes minute, seemingly insignificant objects, dead and inanimate things to which he gives life rather than people and monuments.

37. Guibert, *Parents*, 106.

38. Guibert brings back several characters in several works spanning three decades, creating a kind of auto-intertextuality, but Suzanne and Louise stand out in his texts as real people, part of his autobiography and frequent characters in his texts.

39. "Est fragmentée, comme sans cesse surprise par elle-même, à la recherche de son souffle, refusant obstinément tout emportement lyrique" (De Gaudemar, "Livret," 35).

40. "Plusieurs romans du dix-huitième siècle dès leur préface, se démentaient déjà comme fiction, c'est-à-dire la dédoublaient, et s'énonçaient comme des témoignages réels miraculeusement retrouvés dans quelque grenier, au fond d'une malle providentielle. . . . En se relâchant, l'écriture s'ouvre sur la réalité et tente d'en ramasser des bribes vives" (Blanckeman, *Récits*, 129).

41. Guibert later appeared on a special edition of "Ex Libris," dedicated to his work, hosted by Patrick Poivre d'Arvor, March 7, 1991.

42. Public consciousness about AIDS in the United States was roused at the death of Rock Hudson. During the Reagan years, much confusion existed concerning AIDS, its transmission, and its scope, unfortunately exacerbated by a scientific war largely between Luc Montagnier of the Pasteur Institute in Paris and Robert Gallo of the Center for Disease Control to try to be the first to produce a test for the AIDS virus. In 1985, when Rock Hudson, the manly, charismatic actor and personal friend of the B-movie-star president, was reported to have died of AIDS, the public was shocked to learn of his sexual orientation. That he died of AIDS led to the disease being discussed more openly than it had been previously.

43. Collard was also the star of the film based on the novel, which drew far more attention than the novel, since it received a prize at the Cannes Film Festival awarded as Collard was dying.

44. Duncan, "Gestes," 101.

45. "Surréaliste dans le sadisme" (Breton, *Oeuvres*, 329).

46. The most recent phenomenon involving Sade is a wealth of biographies facilitated by archival material. The brothers Xavier and Thibaut de Sade, descendants of the marquis, allowed Maurice Lever access to their archives to complete his 1993 biography of the marquis, the first work to use these letters and documents. Lever's biography lingers on the role of Donatien's father, his absence and distance, as a presumed cause for Sade's behavior. Francine du Plessix Gray's biography *At Home with the Marquis de Sade* benefited from the same archival material, but she identified the stifling presence of strong, harsh women in Sade's life as the cause of his deviance, trying to create an image of the mother for whom few documents remain. Also published in 1998, as was du Plessix Gray's biography, Lawrence Bongie's biography refuses what he calls attempts at rehabilitation of the marquis's reputation by finding sources for his perversions in his parents.

Although access to previously hidden documents partially explains a plethora of new biographies on Sade, another explanation may be the current need to return to an analysis of the man himself to explain the myth rather than using the myth to explain the darkest side of humankind as did so many of the previous essayists on Sade. Ironically, the writer who masked his own biography has become a prime subject of biographical essay.

The two contemporary Sades, Xavier and Thibaut, are the first descendants to acknowledge their connection to their infamous ancestor. Until the current generation, all other descendants of Sade refused the hereditary title "marquis," since the title had become shorthand for the scandalous Donatien. Instead, the Sade family retained the title "Conte," a title used for a member of a noble family until the time he inherits the estates on the death of his father, at which time the new patriarch assumes in his turn the title "marquis." The current Sades, instead, have once again accepted the title "marquis," signaling their interest in manifesting their lineage to Donatien.

47. "Paradigme dans mon projet du dévoilement de soi" (Guibert, *L'Ami*, 247).

48. "Sa volonté de brouiller les cartes se manifeste aussi dans les récits qu'il écrit: le goût pour l'incognito, les pseudonymes et autres réinventions de soi, représentent une tentative d'échapper à une identité trop limitée; Hervé pratique l'autobiographie tronquée, le journal intime, mais le personage principal est fictif" (Buot, *Hervé Guibert*, 44).

## Chapter 2. Sexual Performance

1. Hayes, *Identity*, 106.

2. Barthes, *Sade*, 147–48.

3. Goffman, *Presentation*, 19.

4. Goffman, *Stigma*, 142–43. Building off Goffman, Gilbert Herdt explains in his anthropological approach to sexuality that at certain times and places

there have been categories that transcend male and female. He sees the multiplicity of genders and of sexes; dimorphism is culturally based (Herdt, "Introduction," 21).

5. Goffman, *Stigma*, 74.

6. Ibid., 79–80.

7. Sedgwick, *Epistemology*.

8. Paglia, *Sexual*, 243.

9. Hayes, *Identity*, 113.

10. Lever, *Sade*, 64

11. Le Brun, *Sade*, 151.

12. Derson, "Narration" and "Théâtralité."

13. Paz, "Erotic," 56–57. In fact Steven Urquhart sees in *Philosphy in the Boudoir* many terms related to sacrifice: "sacrifice," "vengeance," "immolation," "supplice," "châtiment," "offrande," "hommage," and "cérémonie" (Urquhart, "Philosophie," 175).

14. Sade, *Oeuvres*, Vol. 1, 55.

15. Ibid., 56.

16. Corkhill, "Kant," 66.

17. "L'ensemble des illustrations raconte de façon obsédante les violences qui menacent le corps féminin: bastonné, enfermé dans un cerceuil, dénudé et palpé, manié lubriquement, poignardé, dénudé et torturé, décapité, gisant poignardé," (Delon, *Sade*, Vol. 1, 1209).

18. "Sade et ses libraires savaient l'importance de l'image dans la littérature pornographique" (Delon, *Sade*, Vol. III, 1380).

19. Norberg, "Libertine," 250–51.

20. "Donnaient à certaines scènes l'évidence du fantasme" (Delon, *Sade*, Vol. II, xix).

21. This geographic location in California's Death Valley is the lowest point of that valley and thus the lowest point of the United States.

22. Marie Darrieussecq emphasizes the disguises of several of Guibert's characters, such as corrida wear, sexual transvestites' outfits, and so forth (Darrieussecq, "Notion").

23. "Mon corps, soit sous l'effet de la jouissance, soit sous l'effet de la douleur, est mis dans un état de théâtralité, de paroxysme, qu'il me plairait de reproduire, de quelque façon que ce soit: photo, film, bande-son" (Guibert, *Mort*, 171).

24. In a provocative article discussing Hervé Guibert, Michel Foucault, and the medical gaze, Joanne Rendell also notes Guibert's defiance may be a way to resist the medical gaze, a gaze that has objectified, and sometimes punished, the body of the gay man (Rendell, "Testimonial," 33).

25. "L'absence et la trahison, ce qui est normal et ce qui ne l'est pas, le coup de foudre comme initiation au malheur" (Guibert, *L'Homme*, 199).

26. "Du sexe au détour de chaque page" (Buot, *Hervé Guibert*, 143).

27. "Des esclaves rivalisent de plaisirs et de violences en tout genre pour plaire à un maître . . . la cérémonie est racontée dans le moindre détail" (ibid., 143–44).

28. "Tout passe par les mots. Il y a là un travail autour de l'écriture, une joie extrême pour parler des situations limites, une volonté d'aller jusqu'à un point de non-retour dans la mise à nu d'un corps, d'un sexe, d'une vie" (ibid., 144).

29. "Cette indissociabilité du corps, du regard, de la sexualité et de l'autobiographie est exemplifiée par le fait que Guibert, dont les premières publications remontent à 1977, fut critique de photo au journal *Le Monde* également à partir de 1977 . . . Ainsi corps et regard, texte et image sont-ils liés, comme il est dit dans *L'image fantôme*, d'une façon quasi-indissociable, parfois interchangeables" (Brault, "Hervé Guibert," 68–69).

30. "Dans la grammaire qui organise les postures, les épisodes, les scènes, et dans l'invention de la langue, capable de les dire" (Delon, *Sade*, Vol. I, xlvii).

31. Ibid., lii.

32. Barthes, *Camera*, 40.

33. "La plupart des types ont le sida, dans les cuisines baisent sans capote de pauvres filles affamées, en échange d'une grillade de requin congelé" (Guibert, *Fou*, 26).

34. "Ici Hervé Guibert a écrit la plupart de ses livres: *L'Image fantôme, Les Aventures singulières, Les Lubies d'Arthur, Des aveugles, Vous m'avez fait former des fantômes, L'Incognito, Le Protocole compassionnel*" (Guibert, *Protocole*, 150).

35. "La ville, l'Etat, devront désormais ménager un certain nombre de lieux vacants, dans le seul but de petites actions vicieuses, libertines, proprement luxueuses dans les pertes de temps qu'elles occasionneront aux citoyens" (Guibert, *Vice*, 43).

36. One of the photos of nude male mannequins has overtones of an orgy reminiscent of Sade and the illustrations included in some of the editions of his works.

37. Guibert, *Vice*, 61–64.

38. Ibid., 86–88.

39. Carpenter, *Acts*, 49.

40. "Je ferais mieux de décrire des choses que je n'ai pas vues, de me pelotonner comme un aveugle" (Guibert, *Lettres d'Egypte*, 25).

41. Barthes, *Camera*, 85–86.

42. Ibid., 31–32.

## CHAPTER 3. COUNTING THE DAYS

1. Sade, *Oeuvres*, Vol. 1, 65–68.

2. Ibid., 59–63.

3. Cryle, *Geometry*, 121.

4. Ibid., 122.

5. Ibid., 124.

6. Ibid., 126.

7. "Les cuisinières et leurs aides seront respectées, et ceux des messieurs qui enfreindront cette loi payeront mille louis d'amende" (Sade, *Oeuvres*, Vol. 1, 65).

8. Ibid., 380.

9. Cryle, *Geometry*, 130–31.

10. Denneny, "AIDS," 46.

11. "L'origine du voyage remonte au dimanche 14 mars 19 . . ." (Guibert, *Voyage*, 13).

12. "Juste pour pouvoir écrire, pour pouvoir m'écrire qu'il était parti" (ibid., 122).

13. Chambers, *Facing It*, 2.

14. Ibid., 5.

15. Lowe, "Essay," 25.

16. Baldwin, "One-to-One," 7.

17. There are traces of AIDS in early texts, *Blindsight* (1985) or "Les Secrets d'un homme" (1988), a story in the collection *Mauve le vierge* (*Mauve the Virgin*). But an explicit accounting of the syndrome surfaces in 1989 with *L'Incognito* and *Fou de Vincent*. AIDS moves to the center of Guibert's texts with *To the Friend Who Did Not Save My Life* (1990). This corresponds to the history of AIDS in Guibert's own body: he was diagnosed HIV–positive in 1988.

18. "Tu as vraiment la frousse d'attraper le sida, hein" (Guibert, *Fou*, 12).

19. "Je rêve: Vincent me suce, enfin, j'arrive à lui entrer ma bite dans la bouche, je remarque qu'il a sous la langue de petites étoiles blanches, elles ont dû s'échapper du globe stellaire que j'avais laissé allumé pour m'endormir" (ibid., 25).

20. "J'ai des champignons, il disait: j'ai la gale, il disait: j'ai une syph, il disait: j'ai des poux, et j'attirais son corps contre le mien" (ibid., 30).

21. "C'est un champignon qu'il a trop tardé à soigner, je ne dois pas le toucher, ce n'est pas vraiment contagieux, mais il vaut mieux faire attention" (ibid, 67–68).

22. Ibid., 71.

23. "Dans la nuit du 25 au 26 novembre, Vincent tombait d'un troisième étage en jouant au parachute avec un peignoir de bain" (ibid., 7).

24. "Pris tellement de retard dans ce cahier que je dois maintenant raconter deux soirées avec Vincent, dont chacune est un peu l'envers de l'autre" (ibid., 65).

25. "De le retrouver dans ces notes, à l'envers" (ibid., 8).

26. Barthes, "Lover's Discourse," 4.

27. These passages, in a different order, also come to some extent from his journal, recently published as *Le Mausolée des amants*. What concerns me here is *Cytomegalovirus: A Hospitalization Diary* as exemplum of a genre.

28. "Écrire est aussi une façon de rythmer le temps et de le passer" (Guibert, *Cytomegalovirus*, 15).

29. Ibid., 90.

30. "L'écrivain autopathographe s'expose au regard des lecteurs pour trouver une confirmation de son existence après la déclaration de la maladie" (Grisi, *Dans l'intimité*, 218).

31. Anne Hunsaker Hawkins used the term *pathography* to mean "a form of autobiography or biography that describes personal experiences of illness, treatment, and sometimes death" (Hawkins, *Resconstructing*, 1). The term already appears in Oliver Sacks and Freud before it appears in Hawkins, but she first uses it in the way Grisi intends in the passage quoted.

32. The posthumous text *Lettres d'Egypte*, is structured by dated sections except it presents itself as a collection of letters rather than a diary. It is less pertinent to this discussion but will be the object of discussion in later chapters.

33. Guibert had a long-standing relationship with Thierry, a bisexual also involved with Christine, with whom the latter had two children. As Hervé neared

the end of his life, he married Christine in a civil ceremony so that she and her children would benefit from royalties generated by his works. Although at times the triangular relationship proved difficult, Hervé came to admire this woman who shared her man with him.

34. Caron, "Playing," 244.

35. "Je changeai d'angle de prise de vues et, sans rien lui demander, je filmai Claudette Dumouchel. Elle était belle. Je filmai ses longues mains blanches qui pianotaient sur le clavier de l'ordinateur. Je filmai son visage dans cette lumière sublime, j'étais heureux. L'oeil au viseur je voyais que l'image tremblotait imperceptiblement au rythme de ma respiration, des battements de mon coeur. Le mot *End* s'est mis à clignoter dans l'image-témoin. Fin de bande" (Guibert, *Protocole*, 260).

36. Chambers, *Facing It*, 38.

37. Ibid., 39.

38. Denneny, "AIDS," 44.

## CHAPTER 4. IMPRISONED BODIES

1. The text of the other noted libertine Casanova, *Memorie scritte da lui medesimo*, is a picaresque romp through the bedrooms of Europe in tone more lighthearted than Sade. But Sade's texts are ironically comic, as for example when Justine is killed by lightning after surviving voluminous pages of travails. Sade shows us the comic potential of a world upside down as well as a parody of the novel's conventions.

2. "Trois livres en chantier, c'est un peu trop. Mais tant qu'ils resteront en chantier, ils seront un prétexte pour ne pas me tuer" (Guibert, *Mausolée*, 560).

3. Lever, *Sade*, 95.

4. "La sexualité chez Sade ne ressortit pas à la biologie: c'est un fait social; les orgies auxquelles il se complaît sont presque toujours collectives; à Marseille il réclame deux filles et il est accompagné par son valet" (De Beauvoir, *Faut-il?*, 43).

5. "La littérature permet à Sade de déchaîner et de fixer ses rêves, et aussi de surmonter les contradictions impliquées par tout système démoniaque; bien mieux, elle est elle-même un acte démoniaque puisqu'elle exhibe agressivement des fantômes criminels; c'est là ce qui lui donne son prix incomparable" (ibid., 47).

6. Camus, *Rebel*, 46.

7. "Tout dire. Cette seule ligne eût suffi à le rendre suspect, ce projet à le faire condamner, sa réalisation à le faire enfermer. Et il n'y a pas à en rendre responsable le seul Bonaparte. Toujours nous vivons sous un Premier consul, et toujours Sade est poursuivi et à cause de la même exigence: tout dire, il faut tout dire, la liberté est la liberté de tout dire, ce mouvement illimité qui est la tentation de la raison, son voeu secret, sa folie" (Blanchot, *Lautréamont*, 101).

8. "Ce *crime de l'écriture* c'est bien celui dont par son *tout dire* Sade entend se render coupable. Le *tout dire* comme tentative de nomination et de mise en scène exhaustive des signifés de la débauche, du meurtre et de la cruauté produit l'écriture de l'obscène comme double trahison: trahison des codes d'exclusion de la langue de communication par l'accueil des mots vulgaires qui

connotent le peuple et même surtout 'la canaille'; trahison des codes d'exclusion de la langue littéraire par le rejet radical des procédés métaphoriques et de
la convention qui les soutient. Trahison de classe et trahison de culture dans
une corruption généralisée de la langue, le *tout dire* est formellement le crime
qui engendre tous ceux qu'il énonce. C'est le crime sadien par excellence" (Hénaff, *Sade*, 94–95).

    9. Deleuze, *Masochism*, 31–32.

    10. Barthes, *Sade*, 129.

    11. "Qui qualifie ici l'oeuvre, re-présente un espace scénique rivalisant avec
le saint lieu du sacrifice" (Urquhart, "Philosophie," 176).

    12. Quinlan, "Medicine," 246.

    13. "Le lieu du vice est, au niveau le plus profond, le lieu d'un enfermement,
d'un emprisonnement qui, à la limite, n'a pas besoin de murs, comme c'est le
cas, par exemple, pour le crocodile affamé qui est obligé de se donner en spectacle devant des touristes saouls qui le regardent manger" (Sarkonak, "Hervé
Guibert," 59).

    14. "Un récit sadomasochiste, dans l'espoir de lui plaire" (Eribon, "Hervé
Guibert," 7–89).

    15. With its theme of childbearing men, *Les Lubies d'Arthur*, bears a resem-
blance to Apollinaire's *Les Mamelles de Tirésias*. Fecundity is the ultimate triumph over sterility, so Guibert may be creating a fantastic scenario where death
can be cheated.

    16. "On retrouve dans *Les Lubies d'Arthur* ce qui faisait le charme du *Voyage
avec deux enfants:* Cette manière de traiter les mots comme des choses, de les
collectionner avec amour, d'en remplir des tiroirs secrets, de croire à leur chi-
mie" (Brisac, "Petits magiciens,") 18.

    17. "Je me dis que ce livre n'a sa raison d'être que dans cette frange d'incerti-
tude, qui est commune à tous les malades," (Guibert, *A L'ami*, 11).

    18. J'ai eu le SIDA pendant trois mois" (ibid., 9).

    19. "Dans cette chronologie qui cerne et balise les augures de la maladie en
couvrant huit années, alors qu'on sait maintenant que son temps d'incubation
se situe entre quatre ans et demi et huit ans selon Stéphane, les accidents physi-
ologiques ne sont pas moins décisifs que les rencontres sexuelles, ni les prémo-
nitions que les voeux qui tentent de les effacer. C'est cette chronologie-là qui
devient mon schéma, sauf quand je découvre que la progression naît du désor-
dre" (ibid., 62).

    20. "Lorsque le corps de l'écrivain est contaminé, menacé de destruction en
raison de affaiblissement de ses barrages immunitaires, le *corpus* de l'écriture
apparaît à son tour mué, investi comme il est par le péril de la destruction du
centre d'observation privilégié qui lui avait auparavant permis de fonctionner
comme lieu d'ordre et de contrôle" (Bertone, "Mort," 94–95).

    21. In *To the Friend Who Did Not Save My Life,* according to Tom Roach,
Guibert talks about how AIDS changes the dynamic between friends and therefore represents an extension of Foucault's own writings on friendship ("Impersonal," 65).

    22. "Dans le débat, la réponse d'Hervé n'est pas un plaidoyer pour se justi-
fier. Aucun argument, mais un cri: vous ne m'empêcherez jamais de tout écrire,
de tout dire. Dans le combat face à la maladie, il y a un devoir de vérité, un
devoir d'écriture pour se sauver" (Buot, *Hervé Guibert*, 185).

23. Caron, *AIDS*, 141.

24. "Laissai tomber la vérité" (Guibert, *A L'ami*, 175).

25. "C'était un moment difficile, où l'on pouvait penser que l'autre avait des doutes sur la véritable transparence, en cet instant, de votre coeur" (ibid., 177).

26. "La prise de conscience de la maladie et son travail sur le corps et sur l'âme", *Le protocole compassionnel* raconte "l'étonnement et la douleur, la rage et la tristesse d'un homme de trente cinq ans dans lequel s'est greffé le corps d'un vieillard. Mais le bonheur d'une rémission fait une incursion dans le malheur" (Guibert, *Protocole*, book jacket).

27. "La collection de tableaux, cette fièvre du choix, du coup de foudre qui passe à l'hésitation, de la discussion du prix, ce bonheur des rapports ou des contradictions avec les autres tableaux que je possède, cette activité solitaire et fébrile qui me fait parcourir Paris et Rome d'un antiquaire à l'autre et entretenir avec l'un ou l'autre une relation que je trouve très spéciale et passionnante autour de nos désirs, moi de possession, il ou elle de joie ou de bon débarras, dans le deuil de toute activité érotique, l'achat des tableaux est aussi un substitut de sensualité et de présence, car je m'obstine à vivre seul bien qu'on me dise, les médecins et les proches, que ce n'est pas le moment, le tableau diffuse dans l'appartement une présence familière presque corporelle, je dirais que c'est le corps des fantômes qui se diffuse dans les tableaux, la collection de tableaux fomente aussi et entretient cette illusion que je vais continuer de vivre" (ibid., 192).

28. "C'est quand ce que j'écris prend la forme d'un journal que j'ai la plus grande impression de fiction" (ibid., 103).

29. Caron, "Playing," 239.

30. Ibid.

31. "Quand je retrouve une émotion érotique, c'est un peu de vie que je retrouve dans ce bain de mort" (Guibert, *Cytomegalovirus*, 86).

32. "Mais qu'est-ce que j'ai à foutre de foutre à présent?" (ibid., 92).

33. "Guibert nous aura laissé une foison de livres que structure la double problématique du corps et du regard telle qu'elle s'inscrit dans la tension entre autobiographie et fiction. Du corps, Guibert en parle inlassablement, page après page; le corps, le sien ou celui de l'autre, érotisé à son extrême, animé par moments de pulsions les plus perverses, déclencheur des attirances les plus obsessionnelles, et puis aussi, source de répulsion, signe annonciateur d'un pourrissement et d'une mort inévitables. Ce corps, autobiographique ou fictif, c'est le regard qui le compose, qui l'instrumente au fil des passions de celui qui voit ou qui ne voit point, l'amant ou le photographe, le malade ou l'aveugle" (Brault, "Hervé Guibert," 68).

34. "Écrire dans le noir? Écrire jusqu'au bout? En finir pour ne pas arriver à la peur de la mort?" (Guibert, *Cytomegalovirus*, 93).

## CHAPTER 5. DISAPPEARING ACT

1. Sade, *Oeuvres*, Vol. 1, 15.

2. Foucault, *Discipline*, 3–6.

3. Frappier-Mazur, *Writing*, 28 and 29.

4. Quinlan, "Medicine," 236.

5. Sade, *Oeuvres*, Vol. 1, 380–82.

6. Frappier-Mazur, *Writing*, 22.

7. Martyn, *Sublime*, 203.

8. The escape to a castle in the "Black Forest" serves many purposes. We have seen that this location is mythical rather than a reference to a location in the homonymous region of Germany. But moving the party outside France also serves to bring the four friends outside the law and outside the reach of family and friends. The move solidifies the victims' anonymity.

9. "La photographie chez Guibert est toujours un appel non seulement de lumière mais de désir. Elle est toujours une *scène*. Elle entre toujours dans l'articulation syntaxique d'un fantasme" (Saint-Amand, "Mort," 87).

10. "Hervé Guibert, loin de se voir étouffé par les oppressions institutionalisées de l'autobiographie et de l'homophobie détaillées par Sedgwick, cherche plutôt à relever le défi que leurs interpolations lui lancent. Les divers incognitos, pseudonymes et réinventions de soi qui parcourent son oeuvre représentent justement une série de tentatives d'esquiver l'identité néfaste de l'homosexuel, terme que Guibert choisit de considérer comme interdit, mais qui signifie néanmoins chacune des identifcations qu'il invente afin de déstabiliser les tabous de l'homophobie" (Pratt, "Désidentification," 72).

11. Kruger, "Get Fat," 38.

12. Bertone, "Mort," 95.

13. "La diagnostic de la maladie qui marque son corps entraîne aussi un changement radical dans le travail de l'écrivain. La progression du virus alimente paradoxalement le désir de multiplier et diversifier l'oeuvre . . . Hervé est confronté au raccourci vertigineux de sa vie. Il va falloir écrire vite, lutter contre la fatigue, tenter d'obtenir un sursis pour le corps et pour l'écriture. Simplement, avec l'aveu public, le compte à rebours donne l'impression de s'accélérer. Il faut réagir très vite! Le sida devient alors le 'travail' d'Hervé" (Buot, *Hervé Guibert*, 228–29).

14. "Si l'écriture-transfusion et l'immédiateté de la retranscription traduisent une nouvelle étape de la maladie, elle sont aussi liées à l'état singulier du corps du narrateur" (Décarie, "Protocole," 247).

15. Critical discussion of *The 120 Days of Sodom* points out that, especially since the text was written in some haste in the shadow of the impending Revolution and the resultant turmoil in the Bastille, the text remains unfinished. Delon is right, however, to analyze how the text's structure strikes the reader.

16. Lacan, "Kant," 129.

17. Buot, *Hervé Guibert*, 177.

18. "Mais comme toujours, chez Hervé, le paradis des aventures enfantines n'est pas une histoire à l'eau de rose. Il y a aussi une bonne dose d'impudeur, de pulsions, de sauvagerie, de crasse et de sang . . . les deux amis utilisent le sexe, le meurtre, le vol, ils sont tour à tour victime et bourreau. Et puis il y a la mort qui rôde et malgré les mots d'amour d'Arthur, c'est Bichon qui s'en va pour toujours . . . le monde devient lourd, pénible et Arthur résiste comme il peut en arpentant les cimetières pour enlacer les morts" (Buot, *Hervé Guibert*, 178).

19. Pratt, "Autoreprésentation," 147.

20. Sarkonak, "Histoire," 17.

21. "Plus le propos est humainement intenable, plus le teneur de la rhétorique s'impose" (Blanckeman, *Récits*, 137).

22. "A la différence de Sade, dont les fantômes représentaient un exutoire légitime, compensatoire, et surtout imaginaire, les fantômes violemment érotiques de Pirate et de Lune ont été réalisés" (Heathcote, "Erotisme," 194).

23. "S'en prend donc, comme les brigands, à son semblable, son frère: il s'en prend au plaisir à la fois complice et traître de sa propre écriture" (ibid., 195).

24. "Renchérissant donc sur Sade, le texte de Guibert suggère que les 'fantômes' de violence érotique jouissent d'une généralité et d'une popularité qui dépassent de très loin l'enceinte d'un quelconque château de Silling" (ibid., 198).

25. "En présentant, sur le plan textuel comme sur le plan sexuel, une série de doubles jumelés et de membres fragmentés, *Vous m'avez fait former des fantômes* propose—et parodie—une sorte de modèle et de patron du corps masculin, une sorte de vision testiculaire, phalloïde et séminale de la littérature" (ibid., 202).

26. "Une mise à nu de l'érotisation de la cruauté et de la mort" (ibid., 196).

27. "Tandis que les écrits de Sade n'annoncent ni sortie, ni alternative, ni rétribution, le roman de Guibert expose, tout en jouant, son propre délire" (ibid., 194).

28. Saint-Amand, "Mort," 87.

29. "De nombreuses photographies guibertiennes . . . fonctionnent à travers l'invocation d'un monde surréel, même surnaturel, par le biais d'objets qui, selon leur représentation dans l'espace photographique, évoquent une préoccupation avec la capacité des choses à transformer la réalité" (McCaffrey, "Superstition," 24).

30. Grove, "Röntgen's Ghost," 145.

31. Ibid., 142.

32. Ibid., 172.

33. Chambers, *Facing It*, 36.

34. "C'est la télévision choc avec une réalité brute et un spectateur transformé en voyeur" (Buot, *Hervé Guibert*, 255).

35. "Il s'agirait aussi, de voir se mettre en place chez Guibert, parallèlement à la temporalité affolée, un temps de la lenteur, de la reprise au ralenti des choses du quotidien, un temps hors temps qui, il me semble, est davantage inscrit dans la production cinématographique de Guibert ou encore dans les photographies: le temps de l'image fixe. C'est la rencontre de ces deux temporalités, incarnées chacune apparemment davantage dans un médium particulier, dans l'écriture ou dans la vidéo, qui sera ici mise en scène" (Mavrikakis, "L'Oeuvre," 283).

36. "Si l'image parfaite de sa mère au summum de sa beauté, celle de sa tante Suzanne dénudée ou celle du bonheur du monde sont toujours à lire et jamais à voir, c'est parce que 'l'image fantôme se tend [ . . . ] vers autre chose que l'image: vers le récit'" (Worton, "En [d]écrivant," 65).

37. Sarkonak, "Histoire," 10.

38. Mavrikakis, "Bout," 371.

39. "Dans ses récits, Guibert privilégie une narration clinique de sa maladie. Ses textes sont constitués par la répétition et l'accumulation de détails subjectifs sur la multiplicité de ses symptômes, des examens qu'il subit et de ses traitements" (Grisi, *Dans l'intimité*, 155).

40. Apter, "Fantom."

## CHAPTER 6. BODIES IN/AS EVIDENCE

1. Gray, *Home*, 99.
2. Ibid., 413.
3. Lever, *Sade*, 161.
4. Shea, "Sade," 321 and 324.
5. Bongie, *Sade*, xii.
6. Ibid., 182.
7. Ibid., 261.
8. "A voir s'enchaîner de semblables formules, on se dit qu'il y a une lacune dans la raison de Sade, un manque, une folie. On a le sentiment d'une pensée profondément déréglée, suspendue bizarrement sur le vide. Mais tout à coup la logique l'emporte, les objections apparaissent et le système peu à peu se forme" (Blanchot, *Lautréamont*, 20).
9. "Si le crime est l'esprit de la nature, il n'y a pas de crime contre la nature et, par conséquent, il n'y a pas de crime possible. Sade l'affirme, tantôt avec la plus grande satisfaction, tantôt avec la rage la plus vive" (ibid,, 41).
10. "Ainsi l'athéisme, acte suprême de la raison normative, doit instituer le règne de l'absence totale des normes" (Klossowski, *Sade*, 19).
11. Judovitz, "Sex," 171.
12. Norberg, "Libertine," 227.
13. Hunt, "Introduction," 10.
14. Hunt, "Pornography," 305 and 324.
15. Ibid., 330.
16. "Une méfiance plus large à l'égard de l'homosexualité, plus particulièrement à l'égard de la littérature homosexuelle en France" (Genon, "Hervé Guibert en 2004").
17. "La représentation normative, celle de l'identité et de l'opposition, et la déconstruit pour anéantir l'idée d'opposition sans qu'il y ait de conséquences à cela" (Schehr, "Jus," 219).
18. "La quasi omniprésence du corps de Guibert dans l'image invite le spectateur à considérer le corps comme un texte qui fonctionne comme une signature, comme le métonyme du moi" (Ducan, "Gestes," 109).
19. "Fameux dévoilement de soi n'est qu'un prétexte à (re)mettre constamment en scène le sujet en procès qu'il est: en dramatisant, en 'théâtralisant' son moi et son corps (souvent par le biais de miroirs réels ou métaphoriques), il connote une identité à réaliser au lieu de dénoter une identité figée localisable" (Worton, "En [d]écrivant," 70).
20. "Dans un sens, les textes sexographiques de Guibert se conforment aux règles de la pornographie qui exigent l'absence de description de visages, la schématisation des personnages et le manque de logique narrative. Tout comme le pornographe, le romancier transgressif qu'est Guibert force le lecteur à recourir à ses propres expériences pour combler les lacunes et fait donc de lui non seulement son collaborateur ou son co-créateur, mais son complice" (ibid., 70).
21. "Le grand secret que toute son oeuvre répète sans cesse, est que tous les genres sont suspects et que ce n'est qu'en gommant toute distinction générique que l'on construira un érotisme satisfaisant et une ontologie de l'être authentique" (ibid., 75).

22. "Si nous n'avions pas tout dit, tout analysé, comment voudrais-tu que nous eussions pu deviner ce qui te convient?" (Sade, *Oeuvres,* Vol. 1, 69).

23. "Mouvement de tourbillon qui me tire vers la fin (de la deuxième partie) des *Fantômes:* bouclage our bâclage? qui me fait finir en une journée ce que dans le courant habituel du travail j'aurais dû mettre deux ou trois jours à faire, et qui ensuite me laisse triste et bête. Accablement en relisant la première partie, qui me semble assez mauvaise, confuse: dépornographier tout ça? nettoyer chaque phrase? Je repense à Handke, qui a tant confiance au journal—le roman ne porte-il pas vraiment en lui le ratage?" (Guibert, *Mausolée,* 383).

# Bibliography

Apter, Emily. "Fantom Images: Hervé Guibert and the Writing of 'sida' in France." In *Writing AIDS: Gay Literature, Language and Analysis,* edited by Timothy F. Murphy and Suzanne Poirier, 83–97. New York: Columbia University Press, 1993.

Baldwin, Christina. *One-to-One. Self-Understanding Through Journal Writing.* New York: Evans, 1977.

Barthes, Roland. *Sade, Fourier, Loyola.* Paris: Edition du Seuil, 1971. Translated by Richard Miller as *Sade, Fourier, Loyola* (New York: Hill and Wang, 1976).

———. *Camera Lucida. Reflections on Photography.* Translated by Richard Howard. New York: Noonday, 1981.

———. *A Lover's Discourse. Fragments.* Translated by Richard Howard. New York: Hill and Wang, 1978.

Bellour, Raymond. "Guibert ou l'indécidable." *Magazine littéraire,* no. 260 (December 1988): 80–81.

Bataille, Georges. *Littérature et le mal.* Paris: Gallimard, 1990.

Bertone, Manuela. "La mort en soi. L'écriture du sida d'Hervé Guibert." *Franco-Italica,* no. 6 (1994): 89–108.

Blanchot, Maurice. *Lautréamont et Sade.* Paris: Minuit, [1948] 1963. Translated by Stuart Kendall and Michelle Kendall as *Lautréamont and Sade* (Stanford: Stanford University Press, 2004).

Blanckeman, Bruno. *Les récits indécidables: Jean Echenoz, Hervé Guibert, Pascal Quignard.* Paris: Setentrion, 2000.

Bongie, Lawrence. *Sade. A Biographical Essay.* Chicago: University of Chicago Press, 1998.

Boulé, Jean Pierre. *Voices of the Self.* Translated by J. Fletcher. Liverpool: Liverpool University Press, 1999.

———. "Hervé Guibert: création littéraire et *roman faux.*" *French Review* 74, no. 3 (February 2001): 527–36.

Brault, Pascale-Anne. "Hervé Guibert ou le corps du délit." In *Regards sur la France des années 1980: le Roman,* edited by Joseph Brani, Madeleine Cottenet-Hage, and Pierre Verdaguer, 67–74. 1994.

Breton, André. *Oeuvres complètes.* Vol. 1. Paris: Gallimard, 1988.

Brisac, Geneviève. "Les petits magiciens d'Hervé Guibert." *Le Monde,* December 9, 1983.

Buot, François. *Hervé Guibert. Le Jeune homme et la mort.* Paris: Grasset, 1999.

Butler, Judith. *Bodies that Matter. On the Discursive Limits of "Sex."* New York: Routledge, 1993.

Camus, Albert. *The Rebel. An Essay on Man in Revolt.* With a foreword by Sir Herbert Read. Translated by Anthony Bower. New York: Vintage Books, 1956.

Caron, David. "Playing Doctors: Refiguring the Doctor-Patient Relationship in Hervé Guibert's AIDS Novels." *Literature and Medicine* 14, no. 2 (Fall 1995): 237–49.

———. *AIDS in French Culture. Social Ills, Literary Cures.* Madison: University of Wisconsin Press, 2001.

Carpenter, Scott. *Acts of Fiction. Resistance and Resolution from Sade to Baudelaire.* University Park: Pennsylvania State University Press, 1996.

Casanova, Giovanni Giacomo. *Memorie scritte da lui medesimo.* Milan: Garzanti, 1963.

Chambers, Ross. *Facing It. AIDS Diaries and the Death of the Author.* Ann Arbor: University of Michigan Press, 1998.

Collard, Cyril. *Les Nuits fauves: roman.* Paris: Flammarion, 1989. Translated by William Rodarmor as *Savage Nights* (New York: Overlook Press, 1993).

Corkhill, Alan. "Kant, Sade and the Libertine Enlightenment." In *Libertine Enlightenment: Sex, Liberty and License in the Eighteenth Century,* edited by Peter Cryle, 61–74. Busingstoke, England: Palgrave Macmillan, 2004.

Cryle, Peter. *Geometry in the Boudoir. Configurations of French Erotic Narrative.* Ithaca, NY: Cornell University Press, 1994.

Dall'Orto, Giovanni. "'Nature is a Mother Most Sweet': Homosexuality in Sixteenth-Century Italian Libertinism." In *Queer Italia. Same Sex Desire in Italian Literature and Film,* edited by Gary P. Cestaro, 83–104. Article translated by Gary P. Cestaro. New York: Palgrave Macmillan, 2004.

Darrieussecq, Marie. "La notion de leurre chez Hervé Guibert. Décryptage d'un roman-leurre, *L'Incognito.*" *Nottingham French Studies* 34, no. 1 (Spring 1995): 82–88.

De Beauvoir, Simone. *Faut-il brûler Sade?* Paris: Gallimard, 1955. Translated by Paul Dinnage as *The Marquis de Sade. An Essay* (New York: Grove, 1953).

Décarie, Isabelle. "*Le Protocole compassionnel* d'Hervé Guibert: une écriture transfusion." In *French Prose in 2000,* edited by Michael Bishop and Christopher Elson, 241–48. Amsterdam: Rodopi, 2002.

De Gaudemar, Antoine. "Livret d'infamille." *Libération,* May 22, 1986.

Deleuze, Gilles. *Masochism. An Interpretation of Coldness and Cruelty.* Translated by Jean McNeil. New York: George Braziller, 1971.

Denneny, Michael. "AIDS Writing and the Creation of a Gay Culture." In *Confronting AIDS Through Literature: The Responsibilities of Representation,* edited by Judith Lawrence Pastore, 36–54. Urbana: University of Illinois Press, 1993.

Derson, Didier. 2001a. "Narration et didascalies dans l'oeuvre romanesque de Sade." *Revue d'histoire du théâtre* 4 (212): 369–77.

———. 2001b. "La Théâtralité du discours romanesque sadien." *Revue d'histoire du théâtre* 4 (212): 353–68.

*Dorland's Illustrated Medical Dictionary.* 26th edition. Philadelphia: W. B. Saunders, 1985.

Duncan, Derek. "Gestes autobiograhiques: le Sida et les formes d'expression artistiques du moi." *Nottingham French Studies* 34, no. 1 (Spring 1995): 100–11.

Eribon, Didier. "Hervé Guibert et son double." *Le Nouvel observateur* (July 18–24, 1991): 87–89.

Foscolo, Ugo. *Le Ultime lettere di Jacopo Ortis.* Milan: Mursia, 1995.

Foucault, Michel. *Discipline and Punishment. The Birth of the Prison.* Translated by Alan Sheridan. New York: Vintage, 1995.

Frappier-Mazur, Lucienne. *Writing the Orgy: Power and Parody in Sade.* Translated by Gillian C. Gill. Philadelphia: University of Pennsylvania Press, 1996.

Freud, Sigmund. "Contributions to the Theory of Sex." In *The Basic Writings of Sigmund Freud.* Translated, edited, and with an introduction by Dr. A. A. Brill. 553–629. New York: The Modern Library, 1938.

Gallop, Jane. *Intersections: A Reading of Sade with Bataille, Blanchot and Klossowski.* Lincoln: Nebraska University Press, 1981.

Genon, Arnaud. "Hervé Guibert en 2004: état des lieux des études guibertiennes." *Acta fabula,* no. 2 (Spring 2004). http:// www.fabula.org/revue/documents232.php.

Goethe, Wolfgang. *Die Leiden des jungen Werther.* Translated by Elizabeth Mayer and Louise Bogan as *The Sorrows of Young Werther, a Novella* (New York: Random House, 1971).

Goffman, Erving. *The Presentation of Self in Everyday Life.* New York: Anchor, 1959.

———. *Stigma. Notes on the Management of Spoiled Identity.* New York: Simon and Schuster, 1963.

Gray, Francine du Plessix. *At Home with the Marquis de Sade. A Life.* New York: Simon and Schuster, 1998.

Grisi, Stéphane. *Dans l'intimité des maladies. De Montaigne à Hervé Guibert.* Paris: Desclée de Brouwer, 1996.

Grove, Allen W. "Röntgen's Ghosts: Photography, X-Ray and the Victorian Imagination." *Literature and Medicine* 16, no. 2 (Fall 1997): 141–73.

Guibert, Hervé. 1977. *La mort propagande.* Paris: Régine Deforges. Reedited in 1991 with other early texts.

———. *Suzanne et Louise.* Paris: Editions Libres Hallier, 1980.

———. *L'Image fantôme.* Paris: Minuit, 1981. Translated by Robert Bononno as *Ghost Image* (Los Angeles: Sun and Moon Press, 1996).

———. *Les Aventures singulières.* Paris: Minuit, 1982.

———. *Voyage avec deux enfants.* Paris: Minuit, 1982.

———. *Les Chiens.* Paris: Minuit, 1982.

———. *Les Lubies d'Arthur.* Paris: Minuit, 1983.

———. *L'Homme blessé.* With Patrice Chéreau. Paris: Minuit, 1983.

———. *Le Seul visage.* Paris: Minuit, 1984.

———. *Des aveugles.* Paris: Gallimard, 1985. Translated by James Kirkup as *Blindsight* (London: Quartet Books, 1995).

———. *Mes parents.* Paris: Gallimard, 1986. Translated by Liz Heron as *My Parents* (London: Serpent's Tail, 1993).

———. *Vous m'avez fait former des fantômes.* Paris: Gallimard, 1987.

———. *Les Gangsters.* Paris: Minuit, 1988.

———. *Mauve le vierge.* Paris: Gallimard, 1988.

———. *L'Image de soi ou l'injonction de son beau moment?* London: Blake, 1988.

———. *Fou de Vincent.* Paris: Minuit, 1989.

———. *Incognito.* Paris: Gallimard, 1989. Translated by Patricia Roseberry as *Incognito* (Harrogate, England: Broadwater House, 1999).

———. *A l'ami qui ne m'a pas sauvé la vie.* Paris: Gallimard, 1990. Translated by Linda Coverdale as *To the Friend Who Did Not Save My Life.* London: High Risk Books, 1994.

———. *Le protocole compassionnel.* Paris: Gallimard, 1991. Translated by James Kirkup as *The Compassion Protocol* (New York: George Braziller, 1994).

———. *Vice.* Paris: Editions Jacques Bertoin, 1991.

———. *Mon valet et moi.* Paris: Seuil, 1991.

———. *L'Homme au chapeau rouge.* Paris: Gallimard, 1992. Translated by James Kirkup as *The Man in the Red Hat* (London: Quartet Books, 1993).

———. *Cytomégalovirus: Journal d'Hospitalisation.* Paris: Seuil, 1992. Translated by Clara Orban with the assistance of Elliot Weisenberg as *Cytomegalovirus: A Hospitalization Diary* (Lanham, MD: University Press of America, 1996).

———. *Dialogue d'images.* Bordeaux: William Blake, 1992.

———. *Le Paradis.* Paris: Gallimard, 1992. Translated by James Kirkup as *Paradise* (London: Quartet Books, 1996).

———. *Photographies.* Paris: Gallimard, 1993.

———. *Vole mon dragon.* Paris: Gallimard, 1994.

———. *La Piqûre d'amour et autres textes suivi de "La chair fraîche."* Paris: Gallimard, 1994.

———. *Lettres d'Egypte. Du Caire à Assouan, 19 . . .* Arles: Actes Sud, 1995.

———. *Le Mausolée des amants. Journal 1976–1991.* Paris: Gallimard, 2001.

Hawkins, Anne Hunsaker. *Reconstructing Illness: Studies in Pathography.* West Lafayette, IN: Purdue University Press, 1993.

Hayes, Julie Chandler. *Identity and Ideology. Diderot, Sade, and the Serious Genre.* Philadelphia: John Benjamins Publishing Company, 1991.

Heathcote, Owen. "L'érotisme, la violence et le jeu dans *Vous m'avez fait former des fantômes.*" In *Le corps textuel de Hervé Guibert,* edited by Ralph Sarkonak, 189–211. Paris: Lettres Modernes, 1997.

Hekma, Gert. "Sodomites, Platonic Lovers, Contrary Lovers: The Backgrounds of the Modern Homosexual." In *The Pursuit of Sodomy: Male Homosexuality in Renaissance and Enlightenment Europe,* edited by Kent Gerard and Gert Hekma, 433–55. New York: Harrington Park Press, 1989.

Hénaff, Marcel. *Sade. L'invention du corps libertin.* Paris: Presses Universitaires Françaises, 1978. Translated by Xavier Callahan as *Sade. The Invention of the Libertine Body* (Minneapolis: University of Minnesota Press, 1999).

Herdt, Gilbert. "Introduction: Third Sexes and Third Genders." In *Third Sex,*

*Third Gender. Beyond Sexual Dimorphism in Culture and History*, edited by Gilbert Herdt, 21–81. New York: Zone Books, 1996.

Hunt, Lynn. "Introduction: Obscenity and the Origins of Modernity 1500–1800." In *The Invention of Pornography. Obscenity and the Origins of Modernity 1500–1800*, edited by Lynn Hunt, 9–45. New York: Zone Books, 1993.

———. "Pornography and the French Revolution." In *The Invention of Pornography. Obscenity and the Origins of Modernity 1500–1800*, edited by Lynn Hunt, 301–39. New York: Zone Books, 1993.

Judovitz, Dalia. " 'Sex,' Or the Misfortunes of Literature." In *Sade and the Narrative of Transgression*, edited by David B. Allison, Mark S. Roberts, and Allen S. Weiss, 171–98. Cambridge: Cambridge University Press, 1995.

Klossowski, Pierre. *Sade mon prochain. Précédé par Le philosophe scélérat.* Paris: Seuil, [1947] 1967. Translated by Alphonso Lingis as *Sade My Neighbor* (Evanston, IL: Northwestern University Press, 1991).

Kraff-Ebing, Richard von. *Psychopathia Sexualis, A Medico-Forensic Study.* Translated from Latin by Harry E. Wedeck. New York: Putnam, 1965.

Kruger, Steven F. " 'GET FAT, Don't Die!': Eating and AIDS in Gay Men's Culture." In *Eating Culture*, edited by Ron Scapp and Brian Seitz, 36–59. Albany, NY: SUNY Press, 1998.

Lacan, Jacques. "Kant Avec Sade." In *Ecrits 2*, 119–48. Paris: Editions du Seuil, [1962] 1971.

Le Brun, Annie. *Sade. A Sudden Abyss.* Translated by Camille Naish. San Francisco: City Lights Books, 1990.

Lever, Maurice. *Les Bûchers de Sodome. Histoire des infâmes.* Paris: Fayard, 1985.

———. *Sade. A Biography.* Translated by Arthur Goldhammer. New York: Farrar, Straus, Giroux, 1993.

Lowe, Sarah. "Essay." In *The Diary of Frida Kahlo. An Intimate Self-Portrait*, introduction by Carlos Fuentes. Essay and Commentaries by Sarah M. Lowe, 25–29. New York: Abrams, 1995.

Martyn, David. *Sublime Failures: The Ethics of Kant and Sade.* Detroit, MI: Wayne State University Press, 2003.

Mavrikakis, Catherine. "A bout de souffle: vitesse, rage et pornographie. Parcours rapide des textes d'Hervé Guibert et Christine Angot." *The Journal of Twentieth Century Contemporary French Studies* 6, no. 2 (Fall 2002): 370–78.

———. "L'Oeuvre au ralenti: Hervé Guibert ou comment filmer l'air." *Contemporary French and Francophone Studies* 9, no. 3 (September 2005): 283–90.

McCaffrey, Edna. "La superstition dans *Vous m'avez fait former des fantômes.*" *Nottingham French Studies* 34, no. 1 (Spring 1995): 24–31.

Norberg, Kathryn. "The Libertine Whore: Prostitution in French Pornography from Margot to Juliette." In *The Invention of Pornography: Obscenity and the Origins of Modernity 1500–1800*, edited by Lynn Hunt, 225–52. New York: Zone Books, 1993.

Orban, Clara. "Writing, Time, and AIDS in the Works of Hervé Guibert." *Literature & Medicine.* 18, no. 1 (Spring 1999): 132–150.

Paglia, Camille. *Sexual Personae. Art and Decadence from Nefertiti to Emily Dickinson.* New York: Vintage, 1991.

Paz, Octavio. *An Erotic Beyond: Sade.* Translated by Elliot Weinberger. New York: Harcourt Brace and Co., 1998.

Peirce, Charles Sanders. *Peirce on Signs. Writing on Semiotics.* Edited by James Hoopes. Chapel Hill: University of North Carolina Press, 1991.

Poe, Edgar Allen. *The Complete Poems and Stories of Edgar Allen Poe with Selections from his Critical Writings.* Vol. 1. New York: Alfred Knopf, 1971.

Pratt, Murray. "De la désidentification à L'Incognito: à la recherche d'une autobiographique homosexuelle." *Nottingham French Studies* 34, no. 1 (Spring 1995): 70–81.

———. "L'Autoprésentation, l'écriture autre et l'ange." In *Le corps textuel de Hervé Guibert,* edited by Ralph Sarkonak, 133–54. Paris: Lettres Modernes, 1997.

Quinlan, Sean M. "Medicine in the Boudoir: Sade and Moral Hygiene in Post-Thermidorean France." *Textual Practice* 20, no. 2 (2006): 231–55.

Rey, Michel. "Police and Sodomy in Eighteenth-Century Paris: From Sin to Disorder." In *The Pursuit of Sodomy: Male Homosexuality in Renaissance and Enlightenment Europe,* edited by Kent Gerard and Gert Hekma, 129–45. New York: Harrington Park Press, 1989.

Rendell, Joanne. "A Testimonial to Muzil: Hervé Guibert, Foucault, and the Medical Gaze." *Journal of Medical Humanities* 25, no. 1 (Spring 2004): 33–45.

Roach, Tom. "Impersonal Friends: Foucault, Guibert and the Ethics of Discomfort." *New Formations: A Journal of Culture/Theory/Politics* 55 (Spring 2005): 54–72.

Robbe-Grillet, Alain. *Les Gommes.* Paris: Minuit, 1953. Translated as *The Erasers* (New York: Grove, 1964).

Rousseau, Jean-Jacques. *Julie ou la Nouvelle Héloïse.* Paris: Garnier-Flammarion, 1967.

Sade, Donatien, Marquis de. *Oeuvres complètes du Marquis de Sade.* Vol. 12. Edited by Gilbert Lely. Paris: Cercle du Livre Précieux, 1967.

———. *Oeuvres.* Edited with and introduction by Michel Delon. Vols. 1–3. Paris: Gallimard, 1990.

———. *Letters from Prison.* Translated and with an introduction and epilogue by Richard Seaver. New York: Arcade, 1999.

Saint-Amand, Pierre. "Mort à blanc. Guibert et la photographie." In *Le corps textuel de Hervé Guibert,* edited by Ralph Sarkonak, 81–95. Paris: Lettres Modernes, 1997.

Sarkonak, Ralph. "Hervé Guibert: *Vice* des formes." *Nottingham French Studies* 34, no. 1 (Spring 1995): 49–60.

———. "Une histoire de corps." In *Le corps textuel de Hervé Guibert,* edited by Ralph Sarkonak, 5–22. Paris: Lettres Modernes, 1997.

Schehr, Lawrence R. "Jus." In *Le corps textuel de Hervé Guibert,* edited by Ralph Sarkonak, 213–28. Paris: Lettres Modernes, 1997.

Sedgwick, Eve Kosofsky. *Epistemology of the Closet.* Berkeley: University of California Press, 1990.

Shea, Louisa. "Sade and the Cynic Tradition." *Modern Language Quarterly* 67, no. 3 (September 2006): 313–31.

Sontag, Susan. *Illness as Metaphor.* New York: Farrar, Straus and Giroux, 1978.

———. *AIDS and its Metaphors.* New York: Farrar, Straus and Giroux, 1989.

Sorel, Charles. *Histoire comique de Francion.* In *Romanciers du XVIIième siècle. Sorel-Scarron-Furetière-Madame de Lafayette,* 1958 edition, edited by Antoine Adam, 59–527. Paris: Gallimard, 1962.

Steintrager, James A. "Liberating Sade." *The Yale Journal of Criticism* 18, no. 2 (2006): 351–79.

Taylor, Charles. *Sources of the Self. The Making of the Modern Identity.* Cambridge, MA: Harvard University Press, 1989.

Trumbach, Randolph. "Erotic Fantasy and Male Libertinism in Enlightenment England." In *The Invention of Pornography: Obscenity and the Origins of Modernity, 1500–1800,* edited by Lynn Hunt, 253–82. New York: Zone Books, 1993.

———. *Sex and the Gender Revolution.* Vol. 1 *Heterosexuality and the Third Gender in Enlightenment London.* Chicago: University of Chicago Press, 1998.

Urquhart, Steven. "*La Philosophie dans le boudoir:* le boudoir sacrificiel." In *Lire Sade,* edited by Norbert Sclippa, 173–86. Paris: Harmattan, 2004.

Van der Meer, Theo. "The Persecutions of Sodomites in Eighteenth-Century Amsterdam: Changing Perceptions of Sodomy." In *The Pursuit of Sodomy: Male Homosexuality in Renaissance and Enlightenment Europe,* edited by Kent Gerard and Gert Hekma, 263–307. New York: Harrington Park Press, 1989.

Voltaire [François-Marie Arouet]. "Candide, ou l'optimiste." In *Romans et contes de Voltaire,* 180–257. Paris: Flammarion, 1966.

Worton, Michael. "En (d)écrivant le corps en imaginant l'homme, le 'vrai corps' de Guibert." In *Le corps textuel de Hervé Guibert,* edited by Ralph Sarkonak, 63–77. Paris: Lettres Modernes, 1997.

# Index